In refreshingly frank language, Tom Malloy tells it like it is... and like it isn't. *Bankroll* could be the only book you'll ever need to read about independent filmmaking – this book is the real "deal". Tom's energy, enthusiasm and knowledge leap off the page – if this doesn't motivate and inspire you, nothing will!
> — Stephanie Austin, Producer, *Terminator 2,*
> T*rue Lies, Behind Enemy Lines*

Tom Malloy's approach is the real deal and combines pragmatism with a bit of motivational pep talk and spirituality. The book isn't written by a lawyer or ex-agent or trust-fund-gilded producer who happens to be blessed with personal wealth and endless family contacts in high places. Since Tom is a writer, actor, producer, and filmmaker his advice comes from a unique perspective and should be mandatory reading for aspiring film producers.
> — Michael Roban, Executive Producer, *Secretary,*
> *Penelope, Love in the Time of Cholera*

A superb approach to independent financing... an excelling roadmap for the first-time filmmaker.
> — Dov S-S Simens, Author, *From Reel to Deal*;
> Dean, *www.WebFilmSchool.com*

If you want to move from micro-budget films you fund yourself to Indiewood films with budgets between $500K to $7 million, then Tom Malloy's *Bankroll* is absolutely essential reading. Packed with secrets and tricks from a producer who has gotten three films funded and theatrically released in the last two years, *Bankroll* shares amazing ways to get your genre picture made successfully!
> — Jeremy Hanke, Editor-in-Chief, *MicroFilmmaker*
> Magazine; Co-Author, *GreenScreen Made Easy*

The most important part of independent filmmaking is finding the money. Without the money, nothing else can happen. This book tells you how to do it in simple, practical, and effective terms. I've read nothing else as informative on this first and most vital part of getting your film made. Kudos to Tom Malloy.
> — Tom Holland, Writer/Director, *Fright Night,*
> *Child's Play, Thinner*

Malloy's book explores a new approach to finding the funding to make your films. Includes everything you need to know to take those next steps. Highly recommended!

> — Matthew Terry, Screenwriter/Teacher/Director; Columnist for *www.hollywoodlitsales.com*

The simplest, most straightforward instructions I've ever read about how to finance your own film. This isn't an exposé of how studio moguls or bigwig indie producers do it; it's a step-by-step guide to how the hungry, scrappy (but no less savvy) do-it-yourselfers do it. Having read this, I now fully believe that I could go and raise $8 million for my own movie... tonight. (That may be a bit delusional, and easier said than done, but at least I know where to start.)

> — Chad Gervich, TV Writer/Producer and Author; *Small Screen, Big Picture: A Writer's Guide to the TV Business*

Tom Malloy's *Bankroll* outlines unique cutting-edge strategies to make your indie film a reality. It is a must read in this tough economy.

> — Rob Goald, Founder and CEO, Painting with Light Productions; Adjunct Professor of Film at UNLV

When he says that he's not holding anything back, he's not kidding – he tells you everything, including things others won't give away. He gives you ideas on raising money that you can learn at practically any stage in your career.

> — Greg Forston, Senior Vice President Theatrical Distribution, Overture Films

Beginners will appreciate *Bankroll's* comprehensive and prescriptive nature. Filmmakers who have already financed a film or are encountering obstacles along the way will learn to refine and sharpen their strategies. Reading this book and applying its principles will better position you to do what few others can successfully do... find the money.

> — Jessica Creech, *MicroFilmmaker* Magazine

BANKROLL

A NEW APPROACH TO
FINANCING FEATURE FILMS

Tom Malloy

Published by Michael Wiese Productions
12400 Ventura Blvd. # 1111
Studio City, CA 91604
tel. 818.379.8799
fax 818.986.3408
mw@mwp.com
www.mwp.com

Cover Design: MWP
Book Layout: Gina Mansfield Design
Editor: Gary Sunshine

Printed by McNaughton & Gunn, Inc., Saline, Michigan
Manufactured in the United States of America

Library of Congress Cataloging-in-Publication Data

Malloy, Tom, 1974–
 Bankroll : a new approach to financing feature films / Tom Malloy.
   p. cm.
 ISBN 978-1-932907-57-5
 1. Motion picture industry--Finance. 2. Independent filmmakers. I.
Title.

PN1993.5.A1M3255 2009
384'.83--dc22

                                        2008051224

For Emily, Ella, and Tyler,
without whom
I'd be a lot less driven!

CONTENTS

ACKNOWLEDGMENTS

I would first like to thank Bob from Montclair State University, who was my Freshman Writing teacher. Bob's class was like a psychotherapy session. He started by going through all the educational traumas students had been put through by the old-school writing system. When I left his class, I knew I could write.

I would also like to thank all the producers I've worked with and will hopefully continue to work with, including Aimee Schoof and Isen Robbins, Russ Terlecki, Robert Royston, and Sylvia Caminer.

Also, thanks to my parents who really taught me I could achieve anything if I put my mind to it. You hear stories all the time of people succeeding "in spite of" their upbringing. I'm the exact opposite. I fully believe any success I have is "because of" my parents.

Lastly, I really need to thank all the sharks in the film business who have tried to take a bite out of me in the past, screwed me over, or tried to steal from me. Seriously, without the lessons you taught me, I would never have gotten where I am today. I love you all, I forgive you all, and I thank you from the bottom of my heart!

INTRODUCTION

WHO AM I?

Growing Up

My love for the film industry started when I was very young — too young to imagine anything other than fame and fortune in the world of movies. The truth, I'd learn later on, is that film is a *business*, and it's not an easy business! But for most of my early life, from my bedroom in Hunterdon County, New Jersey, all I could visualize were the bright lights and happy faces of Hollywood.

I started as an actor. My first role was playing Captain Hook in my fourth grade production of *Peter Pan* (Peter was played by a female). The years from fifth through eighth grade were hard for me because there was no theater program at our middle school and, hence, I had no outlet. So I resorted to being the class clown, which landed me in the principal's office almost daily.

High school became a busy time for my acting career. I was the star of all the plays and musicals at Hunterdon Central, a fantastic school in Flemington, New Jersey. I had my sights set on the big time!

When it came time to pick a college, I tried to lay the groundwork for my future career. I had heard Montclair University (in Montclair, New Jersey) had a great acting program, and, if I attended, I would be living just minutes from New York City. Perfect. I got accepted as an undergraduate in the theater program right away.

But the program wasn't what I had hoped for. I wasn't interested in classes that were aimed at the least talented people in the room. I needed to excel. So I switched my major to communications and chose film studies as a minor. I didn't know if I was making the right choice. I actually thought I might have ruined my future. Thankfully, a chance meeting in New York City's Little Italy put me back on track.

Gravesend

It was the summer of 1994 and I was sitting with my family outside Il Fornaio on Mulberry Street in Little Italy, despite my protests (I had wanted to eat inside because of the heat, and I had also wanted to eat at a different restaurant). A young waiter named Sal came up to our table and asked, "What can I get you?" My uncle, a jokester visiting from California, replied, "What can we get you?" Sal laughed and responded, "How about some money to make my feature film?"

My ears perked up. "You're making a feature film?" I asked. "Well, I'm an actor." And that was it. My big "discovery."

After several auditions, Sal cast me as one of the four lead roles in *Gravesend*, Sal's semi-autobiographical street film about Brooklyn. What followed were three years of shooting, reshooting, torture, and general hell on earth. There's still folklore associated with the film. I can't attest to all of it, but I will say that we did shoot the movie for $5000, we did tap into street lamps (illegally) to light scenes, and we did do moronic things such as pull up to a gang of thugs on a street corner and ask, "Do you want to shoot a fight scene?" Real fights broke out almost nightly.

But the other actors and I myself were not giving up. I had it especially tough because I was the youngest, and I had no job because I was in college. Getting paid for this movie was out of the question; I've still never even seen a penny from it. I would shoot all night long and then drive back to Montclair from Brooklyn and go to class. Then I'd repeat the process the next night.

My persistence paid off (if not financially). By 1997, *Gravesend* became a hit, kind of. Oliver Stone lent his name as a producer and presented the film. The film had mixed reviews, but some of the most important publications such as *Variety*, the *Los Angeles Times*, and the *New York Times* all raved about it. There are still people out there who consider *Gravesend* the quintessential Brooklyn street film, and the only film to be made in the Cassavettes style in years.

I remember being in Los Angeles in 1998 when *Gravesend* was released to theaters. I foolishly thought I would be returning to New York City to find a mailbox full of scripts. I was wrong.

Gravesend made me a "hot item" for about thirty days. And then, as fast as it came, it was gone. In that short period I got some of the best auditions in the world, but the roles kept going to established actors who were already famous. Looking back, I believe one of my errors was not hiring a publicist. But hindsight is 20/20, and I soon found myself without an agent, without a job, and without a prayer, living in New York City.

The Next Step

There aren't many jobs for out-of-work actors besides restaurant-industry positions. I had a special talent, though. I'd been a computer expert my whole life and I knew how to make money doing it. So that became my "support until" job.

I've always hated the term *fall back*. People told me for years that I needed a career to "fall back on." What a horrible phrase! It implies you are "falling" and going "backward." I made the conscious decision in those hard times in New York to change the phrase to "support until." This way, I could look at any job and simply say, "This job is *supporting* me *until* I make it in the film business."

SIDE NOTE

I realized rather quickly that the only way to get what I wanted in the movie world was to try to learn every aspect of it. My free time was spent reading industry books, watching videos, and talking to people, all to get knowledge of the business in which I wanted so much to work.

During those six to seven years, I became a very strong writer through much hard work and persistence. At the time of this publication, I've optioned, sold, or had movies made from eight of the twelve scripts I've written. I'm now in the Writers Guild of America (WGA) and have made lots of money through my writing.

In the meantime, I also started to realize that the person who holds all the cards is the producer... and not just any producer. More specifically, the producer who had the money or controlled the money. This would become an important discovery.

AnySwing Goes

Around the summer of 2002, I wrote a movie called *AnySwing Goes*, a dance film/romantic comedy. I created the lead role of Ethan specifically for myself. I had been taking dance lessons in West Coast Swing, a bluesy, slinky form of swing that's danced to hip-hop, R&B, pop, and country. I was getting pretty good, so I figured this movie could showcase my multiple talents. More than that, I assumed that knowledge of dance gave me job security. If they tried to cast Matt Damon in my role, I could fight back and say, "He can't dance like I can!"

Right away I optioned *AnySwing Goes* for $10,000 to a producer who supposedly controlled these big investors who were going to invest $2 million into the film. I was so wide-eyed and innocent, I would have signed any contract and given away any rights, as long as I got to play that role. And that, unfortunately, is what I did.

I'll save you the horribly depressing details and just condense it to this: The producer (who never had money to begin with) screwed me and lied to me in every way possible for the next three years. He continually dangled the carrot that the movie was "just about to start." He'd tell me July, and once July came, he'd tell me September. Once September came, he'd tell me January. And, like a fool, I kept believing in him and hoping and praying that he was going to make my film. He eventually tried to steal the script and make it his own, and kick me out of the project. I didn't have any money to sue him, so I basically walked away and let him self-destruct, which he did, several months later. Finally, everyone involved knew he was a liar.

Though it was a personal victory, it didn't help me financially. It was 2005. I had no job (except for the little computer gigs I would do here and there), and now I found out that my wife, whom I had been married to for about six months, was now pregnant.

The Attic

Desperation can lead to great things. My whole life, I had been an avid fan of scary and horror movies, so I figured I would abandon the mess of *AnySwing* and write a thriller. Within one month, I completed a script for *The Attic*, a psychological thriller about one girl's haunting in the midst of family troubles. By the end of the next month, I had Mary Lambert, the director of *Pet Sematary*, attached to direct.

Now I needed the money. I had written the script with a budget in mind (one location), and I would play the third lead. But what was I to do? I had a pregnant wife, no job, and a burning desire to make a movie. I also had an established director attached in a proven genre, and I had a great script. I had to get my hands on $500,000 to make this movie.

Thankfully, in that following month, I learned to raise money.

Sure, I've refined my fundraising techniques since then, but 90% of what I still use today came out of the situation I was in back in 2005.

I learned to take the bull by the horns. I needed $500,000, and no one was going to raise that money for me. I had a dream, and I desperately felt the need to make it a reality. And that's what I did.

The Result

And now, over three years later, things have changed. I've now raised over $15 million for three feature films, a documentary, and an educational video. I live in a dream house in the hills of Studio City, California. People come to me for advice all the time, and I get scripts submitted to me daily. I have multiple projects in development, and get my phone calls returned from everyone except the really, really high ups or the rude people (whom I really don't want to talk to anyway).

After *The Attic*, I raised over $2 million for *The Alphabet Killer*, a psychological thriller I wrote that was based on a true series of unsolved murders that took place in Rochester, New York (where we ended up shooting the film in early 2007). The film was directed by Rob Schmidt (*Wrong Turn*), and stars Eliza Dushku, Tim Hutton, Cary Elwes, me!, Michael Ironside, and Bill Moseley.

After *The Alphabet Killer*, I, along with my producing partner at the time, raised over $5 million for *Love N' Dancing*. This was a brand new dance film (written by me), which had a completely different story than *AnySwing* (which is still on a shelf, somewhere). *Love N' Dancing* was shot in late 2007, directed by Rob Iscove (*She's All That*). The film stars Amy Smart, me!, Billy Zane, Betty White, and Rachel Dratch.

I'm kind of an anomaly. I'm an expert at film financing who only wants to utilize these skills for a specific purpose.

I've been asked by several companies to come on board and be their finance guy, but I've turned down almost every offer. People who know me know that I have the ability to finance films, but I only wish to do so if there's something in the project that excites me — namely, a good role to play! That's where the anomaly part comes in: The actor in me has to be satisfied, or I'm not interested in putting my time and effort into a project and hitting up my money connections. But that should have no effect on you, the reader.

You might be strictly a producer, a producer-writer, a producer-director, a producer-writer-director-actor (yikes!), or any combination/permutation of those roles. At the end of the day, money is the only thing that will get your film made, whatever job you wish to take. You could use the techniques in this book to raise money and then become the caterer (though I'd take a hefty finder's fee if I were you). It's all about getting it done.

I've always believed in karma. I feel that if you put enough good karma out there, it will come back to you. One of the ways I did this was to keep myself available to anyone who wanted to talk to me with questions about the film business. I can sense the desperation of these young filmmakers (sometimes they're not so young). I've been there, and I want to give all the help I can.

My wife and I have been married for five years, and we now have two kids, a daughter who's three and a half, and son who just turned two. In addition to my work in the film business, for the past six years, I've been a motivational speaker for kids for A Vision in Motion, a speakers' bureau in New Jersey. I tell the kids how to be positive and stay away from drugs, something I've done my whole life. Since my schedule is pretty crazy, I can only speak one week a semester, so for that week the bureau flies me out and packs as many speeches in as they can (I once did sixteen speeches in eleven days).

I work pretty much non-stop, and my wife, whose full-time job is being a mom, works equally as hard, if not harder. So it was no wonder she would roll her eyes whenever I'd tell her I was going to the local diner to meet with another hopeful filmmaker who wanted some advice. (The joke is, most of the time the people made me pay for the lunch because they were broke!)

To have more time for my family and my work, I decided to put all of my techniques into a book. I've succeeded in raising money for films, and I know you want to do the same. I'm not holding anything back. I'm revealing all the techniques and tricks I use so that you, too, can make your dream a reality. It's not easy to raise money for your film. But it can be done. Here's how.

WELCOME TO INDIEWOOD

1

Welcome

Welcome to Indiewood. Indiewood doesn't have a geographical location, but it does have a place: It exists outside the Hollywood studio system. Sure, in the past, Hollywood has dabbled in Indiewood, but those mini-majors (Sony Pictures Classics, Focus Features, etc.) are just little versions of the big distributors. When I talk about Indiewood, I mean truly making a film from scratch and then trying to sell it to one of those big Hollywood distributors for a theatrical release.

Indiewood is where I live. It's how I support my wife and two kids, and how I pay for my house and cars. I have friends in the Hollywood system who make double or even triple the money I do per year, but, for what it's worth, they respect the hell out of me and want to be doing what I do.

What I do is risky, exciting at times, mostly difficult, and has so many ups and downs it can be compared to crack addiction. As Indiewood producers, we are all "chasing the crack high" — that great feeling you get when a film is financed and you are in production. There's a little bit of a high in preproduction, and a little bit of a high in postproduction (sometimes), but the time where you are loving life 24/7 is when you are shooting.

Granted, there are tough times during production and disasters happen (we almost blew up an entire block in Spencerport, New York, when we were filming *The Alphabet*

Killer), but production generates a feeling that I cannot explain — you have to experience it for yourself. Everything is so fantastic until production ends.

Then reality hits and you have to sell a movie and make money. If the film makes money, you can use your private equity investors to do another film. If the film doesn't make money, you just burned your investors and you better start looking for new ones.

This is a world where everyone talks a great game. All the players have various projects in different stages of development, but most (and I'm talking north of 90%) are just "chasing the high." They're not gonna get there.

Technology, especially the recent advent of digital cameras that cost next to nothing and produce amazing results, has opened the floodgates. Any wannabe filmmaker with $25,000 can make a movie that has the potential to look good. The unfortunate side effect is that, 99% of the time, these movies are very bad, and they impose a negative stamp on the indie film world. They tell an investor, "Invest in independent films, and you're gonna lose money."

In Indiewood, budgets range from $300,000 to $8 million. A viable movie can be made for $300,000. Going over $8 million would be foolish; at that point, you should just work with a studio. But these movies that fall within this range are not made by students and are not cheaply done. They have union crews (as many as can be afforded), always deal with the Screen Actors Guild (SAG) (*never* make a non-SAG movie), most of the time deal with the WGA, and almost always deal with the Directors Guild of America (DGA) (unless I'm breaking in a new director I think is a hidden talent).

Some may disagree with my numerical definition of what constitutes an independent film, but that range I stated above is the one I'm addressing in this book. If you want to raise $10,000, I guess you could use some of the techniques in here, but most of them don't apply. If you want to raise $15 million, again, some of the techniques may work, but a lot of them aren't going to help you.

However, if you have a movie that falls within that $300,000 to $8 million budget, you're going to want to listen.

My First Project as a Producer

In 2001, I made an educational video called *The Agony of Ecstasy*. It was funded by a recovering alcoholic who wanted to give something back to the world. He advanced us $3000 and asked us to shoot a video geared for high schools.

My producing partner at the time and I took the $3000 and used our Canon XL-1 (mini-DV) camera, which was one of the top prosumer cameras back then. We set out to make an indie-type street film instead of the moronic drug videos that are out there, so many of which we watched in preparation for producing our film. One video about crack featured interpretive dancers in ballet uniforms. We were crying as we watched it!

We took to the streets of New York and did on-camera interviews, and we even got into an actual rave party, a feat that VH1 couldn't even achieve for their ecstasy special. Our video came out quite well.

Once we finished the video, we started selling it to schools through various distributors. I didn't know it at the time, but educational videos sell for big numbers. The lowest price I saw the video go for was $99. Most of the time it was $129.99, and sometimes it was $200, if I included a CD containing a little PowerPoint presentation and test for the class that I made up from the knowledge I gained while shooting.

Well, our video sold to over a thousand schools. All in all, it's probably made over $150,000. Out of that, I've probably seen around $10,000. But, it was the first little film I ever produced, and it made money.

My first produced project that made money! An educational video for high schools. This was the video box cover I designed.

I remember talking to a distributor from Pyramid Media, one of the distributors of the video (I believe you can still buy it there). He told me that, back in the day, educational videos could make millions. Nowadays, the market was flooded.

That was the first time I heard about how great it "used to be," but it wouldn't be my last.

Unfortunately, "things used to be so much better" has become the battle cry of the independent film world. Each year, *Variety* and the *Hollywood Reporter* love to report how the American Film Market (AFM) was the "slowest yet," and at Cannes, "No one is buying…" and at Toronto the "market is grim."

Is it true? Somewhat. I'll go into more detail as I explain the three features I produced over the past two years.

The Attic

This was the first time I experienced the "crack high." When we were shooting *The Attic*, we really thought it was going to be the next *Halloween*. I felt I knew enough about horror movies (being a horror movie junkie my whole life) to be able to craft the scariest movie of all time.

The problem was, it's not that easy. And, it wasn't just me doing the crafting. Early on, I had been in talks with an editor/wannabe director (let's call him "the WBD") who wanted to direct *The Attic*. He was, funny enough, the same guy who had been attached to direct *AnySwing Goes*, and he was getting screwed over by that scum producer ("the SP") as well.

About two years into the *AnySwing Goes* fiasco, I felt a connection with this guy. I thought that, together, we were fighting this SP. I told him that I was getting a movie funded, and I wanted him to direct. He immediately read the script for *The Attic* and jumped in. He started doing his own rewrites, which I shouldn't have let happen. I wasn't yet WGA and didn't know that this isn't how it's done.

In the meantime, as I explained in the introduction, once I started to expose the con-man SP, he tried to push me out of the film. What I didn't know was that this guy, the WBD, was supporting him. Looking back on it, I realize he was doing it out of fear for his own job. He thought that the SP was going to be successful and that I was just a kid. He was wrong. The SP has never done any film project to my knowledge (or IMDb's knowledge), and I now live in a house that they both could only dream of owning.

When I discovered this bit of intrigue, I quickly lost interest in his directing *The Attic*. On top of that, I had partnered up with other producers, and choosing a director wasn't my sole decision. I gave a lot of my power away on that film because I was so young and naive. I had brought pretty much all the money... I should have had the most control! (I realized that soon enough, and made up for this on my second film.) But, it was probably worth it because I did have a lot to learn.

So I took it upon myself to remove the WBD's changes from my script. The problem was, as he was making changes, I was making changes, and I couldn't remember which were his and which were mine. Truly, I tried to take everything out, but I just couldn't tell for sure.

This guy, upon hearing that the film was financed and he wasn't the director, was furious! He threatened to sue unless I gave him shared credit on the film. As another insult, he directed all his comments to my producing partners because, as he put in an email, "Tom is just a child and a thief." I couldn't believe it! He had already put the knife in my back on *Any-Swing Goes*. Now, in the case of *The Attic,* he actually thought I was trying to steal his writing because it was so good!

I hired my own attorney to make sure the WBD didn't get shared credit. The joke is, the WBD probably changed 15% of the script, and never changed one scene from my original draft. He only changed dialogue, which, according to the WGA, doesn't warrant a credit. So even if I kept all his stuff in there, he wouldn't have had a case. But I wasn't WGA, and I didn't know this yet.

The attorney I hired was a kind of arrogant, eternally pissed-off New York City lawyer. Looking back on it, he screwed me somewhat. He could have told me the day I met him exactly what I had to do to get this guy out of my script, but instead he fed it to me piecemeal over the next four weeks. I recognize this now as typical lawyer BS… a strategy for running up an hourly tab. We had signed Mary Lambert at that point, and we started to get cast attached.

I eventually found out this lawyer's plan was simple:

◊ Take out anything from the script that I even remotely considered might not be mine, and put "…" in its place.

◊ Copyright that script.

◊ Have a brand-new writer who knows nothing about the script come in and fill in those blanks.

After I completed this, the WBD wouldn't have a case. Realize that I just told you, the reader, how to do this in fifteen seconds. This lawyer slowly fed it to me, and by the time he got to what I had to do, I felt it was too late.

On top of that, I started feeling a bit bad for the WBD. His marriage was falling apart, and, truthfully, he had been screwed by the *AnySwing Goes* producer (SP) as well (though he chose his side and it was the wrong one to choose). The only thing I was really pissed at was his anger toward me. So, I said, "Forget it," and gave the guy a shared writing credit. I remember this really bothered me because I thought *The Attic* was going to be so big! I didn't want people thinking that the dialogue being said on the screen was his. I did everything in my power to remove what I thought was his writing from the script, but there are still one or two lines in the finished product that I'm unsure about. So, for those one or two lines, he's got a shared credit. It just shows what karma gets you. The WBD hasn't written anything since, he's not in the WGA or the DGA, and he's getting up there in age. My bet is that he'll never write or direct for the screen.

The lesson is, always try to do the right thing. It helps so much in this business. Karma comes around. Good deeds get paid back. Screwing someone over, well, that comes back too.

Not to say there aren't two sides to any story. In all fairness, I bet if you heard this guy's version, he might blame it all on me. Probably not, though. The facts are very clear. I tried to reason with him several times. The only case that he could argue is that maybe there were more than one or two lines in the movie that were still his (but I'd love him to point out which ones). That still doesn't warrant shared credit.

When I first started getting *The Attic* together, I was afraid of the SP from *AnySwing Goes*. He really gave off this air that he was a powerful producer. I look back and laugh at this. He had everyone bowing to him because he was a complete con artist, and he was good at it. I'm thanking him officially, because I've since run into several con artists, and I've always been the first one to pick them out.

Aimee Schoof and Isen Robbins had been attached to *AnySwing Goes* as producers. At first, the SP was adamantly against hiring them. I never quite knew why, but I now think it's because he knew they would eventually weed him out as a fraud.

SIDE NOTE

You'll notice something in this book. For those I like and respect, I use their real names. Others, however, are referred to as "that guy" or "that woman," or they get nicknames like the WBD and the SP. Exception to the rule: I identify all my investors as "HNI" (High Net-Worth Individual). I love them all, but they don't want their names plastered everywhere!

Aimee and Isen are good New York indie producers. They can get the job done at any budget and can be hard with numbers, which sometimes crews and vendors hate, but investors love. I met them because they were hired to produce *Any Swing Goes*, and eventually, they got screwed over by the same producer (the SP). I'll always remember the day Isen called me, though, and gave me the heads up that the SP was trying to boot me out of the movie and steal my script. Isen chose the winning team, and that will stick with me forever.

I really liked Aimee and Isen from the start and wanted to use them for *The Attic*, but I didn't want this fake SP knowing about it, because I still thought *Any Swing Goes* might happen.

So I went out and got two different producers to help with *The Attic*. Mistake. One was a lawyer, who, despite acting negative all the time, was not a bad guy and has done some okay stuff. The other was a director who was bitter and arrogant. Right away, the three of us didn't mix. The funny thing is, this was when I was considering hiring the WBD to direct *The Attic*. I didn't realize it then, but they were trying to re-move the WBD and replace him with the arrogant director guy. (Ironically, when the WBD threatened to sue me, he went right to this lawyer for advice. I guess he didn't realize that the lawyer was trying to screw him a few months earlier.) This di-rector thought he was the God of indie film, though I'd never heard of any movie he claimed to have made. He thought of me as just an actor who didn't have any special film ability.

I knew I was going down a bad path with them but was willing to stick it out. At that time, the fake SP found out I was making another movie and used it as the perfect excuse to get angry with me. I still don't know how I accepted this. He said, "How could you do this to me?" I actually felt that I had done something wrong. Ridiculous! Back then, I believed the SP thought I looked up to him and wanted him on every project I did, but I know now that's not true. He was just creating something out of nothing so he could boot me out of *AnySwing Goes* and continue the charade. Aimee and Isen were the ones who eventually called him out and exposed him, but I was booted off the project long before then.

Anyway, the SP, who was the main opponent to Aimee and Isen when they were hired for *AnySwing Goes*, now was "appalled" that I didn't choose them to produce *The Attic*. The joke is, I didn't even realize that was an option, and I would have attached them without hesitation. I balked out of fear that the SP would retaliate, and now here he was telling me I should do it. It's a classic example of the con artist's technique. He tries to make you look like you did something wrong, no matter what.

I was forced to join the two producers I hired (the lawyer and the director) with Aimee and Isen, and the kitchen had even more cooks. On top of that, I really started thinking that the arrogant director was going to try to take over *The Attic*. All I could think of was that it was going to be *AnySwing Goes* all over again, where I'd be booted out. So, I made a judgment call and asked the lawyer and director to step away from the project. They did so without much fanfare, though I had to pay them $5000, as the lawyer had put together some boilerplate paperwork.

SIDE NOTE

I've run into the lawyer since then, and we're amicable to each other, but I've never again seen the director guy, and I'm pretty sure he hates my guts. I would only assume this because I found out later he *did* want to take over the project and direct. So I'm sure there's bad blood. But, like the late Bernie Brillstein said, "You're nobody in this town until someone wants you dead."

The Attic moved forward with Aimee and Isen joined by a producer named Russ Terlecki, who was able to bring $90,000 or so from various sources (on top of the initial $250,000 that I had raised).

I'm not going to go into too much detail about how the film turned out, because this book focuses on the funding of films, not the execution or the distribution, but I will bring up a few relevant points.

I learned two amazing lessons while shooting *The Attic*. The first is perhaps one of the most important rules I know: *The absolute best time to raise money for a feature film is when you are in production.* I'll go more into this in Chapter 13: The Dangerous Approach. But just know now that the lights, camera, and action of a movie set make investors open their pockets.

We needed about $550,000 to complete *The Attic*, and, thankfully, I raised the gap (around $200,000) as we were shooting. I had pitched and sold a great guy and his dad, who owned an upstate New York Internet company that was taking off. (They recently sold the site for $40 million, I believe.) They invested $75,000, and found someone else to match their funds. So now we had around $490,000. When we were done shooting and were in post, I went back to the Internet guys and they graciously gave us another $25,000. Because we had a film shooting, they invested.

Second lesson I learned was a little more intricate. There's a great book I recommend for any film producer called *From Reel to Deal* by Dov S–S Simens. When people express an interest in becoming film producers, I tell them to begin there. Dov started many careers, including Quentin Tarantino's. He breaks down a section where he answers the question, How do you make a $200 million film? His response is, Make a $20 million film that is successful. How do you make a $20 million film? Make a $2 million film that is successful. How do you make a $2 million film? Make a $200,000 film that is successful, and so on. You get the picture?

One of the few points I disagree with in Simens' book is his use of the phrase "that is successful." I have found that if you want to make a $2 million film, you only need to have

Photo by Scott Sloan

Director Mary Lambert giving me last-minute tips on the set of The Attic.

made a $200,000 film. It doesn't have to have been successful. You just have to have done it.

Let me explain. Suppose you were starting a dance club. Wouldn't you rather have the pro designing the space be someone who had designed clubs in the past? Maybe he designed the XYZ club and that club failed. Is it this one person's fault? Probably not. Other factors play important roles in the club's success. The key is that you've hired someone who has experience doing the job you need accomplished.

Think about how that relates to film: I realized, after we had finished *The Attic*, that I had a little cachet. I had completed a film for $550,000. I had already lined up another project called *The Alphabet Killer*, and this time I needed over $2 million. Not only had *The Attic* not made money at that point, we hadn't even screened it for a distributor. But, the movie was done, and that's when I learned a second great lesson: You start making movies, and it's way easier to get more movies going.

The Alphabet Killer

In 2005, my wife Emily and I were living in New Jersey, just after the birth of our daughter, Ella. I told Emily that I wanted to write another scary movie, but this time make it more of a true crime/psychological thriller. Right away, she remembered a story about an unsolved serial killer case that took place in her hometown of Rochester, New York. Apparently, in the early 1970s, a man killed three young girls, aged ten through twelve, who each had the same first and last initial, then buried them in the town corresponding to that initial. For instance, the first victim, Carmen Colon was buried in Churchville. The case remained unsolved, and the culprit was referred to as the Double Initial Killer.

"The Double Initial Killer" sounded like a weak title for a movie. Also, the real killings involved three letters, not two (the first name, the last name, and the town name).

So I called the project *The Alphabet Killer*. (Funny enough, when there was a break on the case a year ago, CNN referred to it as The Alphabet Killer, which was a name I created!) I also decided to set the script in the present day, to avoid dealing with the budget additions that come with shooting a film set in the 1970s.

I also decided to stay away from the crimes' victims. I didn't want to focus on young girls being murdered, so I made the main focus of the story an internal battle going on inside lead investigator Megan Paige (eventually played by Eliza Dushku). I chose schizophrenia because many schizophrenics have a lot of trouble with letters and numbers.

I did a ton of research. It turns out, luckily, that the mother of my sister-in-law's then-boyfriend was a police investigator and had worked on the case, which gave me my first big "in." I also read a lot about schizophrenia and spoke with several psychologists.

The scope of the film was a lot bigger than *The Attic*. It was a really gripping crime thriller that took place throughout all of Rochester, so I knew it could not be done as cheaply. I went back to my production team on *The Attic* and brought them on board. We calculated that the film would have to be shot for at least $2 million.

Great. I had my number. Now I had to go raise it.

The main HNI involved with the picture was a friend from my network who had given $75,000 to *The Attic*. He was a big fan of true crime stories, and had ties with the local and state police of Rochester. He was a big figure in the Rochester community as well, and became a very valuable resource during filming.

But he needed to be convinced to write a $2 million check, because the $75,000 he had invested in *The Attic* had not come back to him, and there's a big difference between that figure and $2 million! In fact, not even a fraction of his initial outlay had come back. Nothing.

I was able to get some initial funding from my Internet HNI to the tune of $25,000, which allowed us to start some development of the film (see Chapter 12: The Attachment Approach). In the end, however, continual trips up to Rochester pitching this guy on the viability of the project, and lots of nights drinking together, closed the deal.

I attached director Rob Schmidt, whose last film, *Wrong Turn*, had made $51 million in theaters and DVD sales and rentals. How did I do this? Well, I was looking for an editor to recut *The Attic*, and I emailed Rob through his website. I wanted to talk to his *Wrong Turn* editor. We actually had offered Rob the directing job on *The Attic*, but the project wasn't right for him at the time. Rob gave me the name of the editor and let me know that he had great admiration for my *Attic* script. I emailed him back right away, saying, "Well, I've got another one, if you're interested!" He was, and, within forty-eight hours of my mailing him the screenplay for *The Alphabet Killer*, he was attached.

During a trip up to Rochester, I learned one of the most valuable tricks for convincing an investor to invest. This could truly be considered "underhanded," but I swear that I did it with pure innocence. My mother-in-law worked for NBC News in Rochester, and I asked her to see if she could get a story for us on the making of the film (though it was a way off). I figured it would inspire local interest and perhaps drum up some money.

My mother-in-law set up the interview, and I invited the HNI to join me. Well, the local Rochester news did a fantastic story that featured me as the writer-producer and my HNI (whose name is Greg) as the executive producer. I really thought innocently that it would just serve to get him excited about the film and make a stir in the community.

Unexpectedly, I got a call from Greg about a week later. "Everyone is blowing up my phone! They keep asking me when the movie is going to be shot!" The strangest thing happened... he practically had to go ahead with the film or risk losing face!

We started assembling the elements and eventually delivered Greg a kickass package. We hired Kelly Wagner and Nancy Nayor to cast the film, who had cast *Hostel*, *The Grudge*, *The Grudge 2*, and *The Exorcism of Emily Rose*. We went after a lot of A-list talent to play Megan, the lead character, who basically carries the film. Rob Schmidt had suggested we consider Eliza Dushku. She liked the script, and it turned out to be a good fit. After Eliza signed on, the rest of the cast fell into place (this usually happens after one star says yes), and Tim Hutton, Cary Elwes, and Michael Ironside all came on board. I need to mention that several of the actors, including Ironside, Bill Moseley, and Martin Donovan, signed on primarily because they were Rob's friends. That goes to show what hiring an experienced director does for your project.

We were about two months away from our intended shooting date. Unfortunately, my HNI thought we were going to be able to raise the $2 million through other sources, and he had only committed about $300,000 so far. I'll go over exactly what happened in later chapters, but this was a mistake I made. The other producers thought, "Well, Tom's handling it," so they all sat around and waited for the HNI to close. Thank God he did, but it took many trips and many drinks.

When he finally put the check in, we were literally two weeks away from principal photography. I remember being at his playhouse (he actually had a separate house for his cars and games) with the rest of the producers, and going through the exact same pitch that I had been working on him for months. At one point, he left the room with his father-in-law and we were all sitting there, wondering if we were going to have to tell everyone that the movie was to be shut down. He came back in, his face giving nothing away at first, and then sat down and said, "Let's make a movie."

It was one of the greatest feelings of my life, but I wouldn't wish that stress on anyone. Every day I went into the production office wondering, "Is this the last day I'll be here?" Ughh… it's a terrifying feeling.

But Greg came through like a champ, and the movie, I believe, came out amazing.

In the meantime, I was busy trying to finance my third film in two years. It was the dance film that I always wanted to do, and it would be the most commercial film I had ever made. There were two major obstacles: 1) We needed $3 million, which would eventually balloon to over $7 million, and 2) I was going to be the star.

Love N' Dancing

I could write an entire book on the trials and tribulations of *Love N' Dancing*. However, for the purposes of this book, I'm going to focus on the money-raising aspects of this film and the lessons that I can pass on to you.

When I realized that *Any Swing Goes* was never going to happen, I shelved the project several years prior to writing *Love N' Dancing*, which I started in 2006. The only similarities are that there's dancing in both. I went back to the first time I ever saw West Coast Swing, way back in 1998. There was a dance competition called The Big Apple Country Dance Festival (that still exists, I believe). I was watching the professional Jack & Jill Competition, where competitors don't know their partners or the music… they have to create a routine on the spot.

I watched this big guy, John Lindo, dance. He was over three hundred pounds and he was fantastic. I was so blown away by the style of dance that I said two things:

◊ I've got to make a movie about West Coast Swing.

◊ I've got to put that big guy in it.

When I wrote *AnySwing Goes*, the dancing was a subplot. In *Love N' Dancing*, West Coast Swing would take center stage.

A funny thing happened that night in 1998. When they announced the winners, John Lindo took second place. I was awestruck, along with the crowd. Then they announced the winner and he went out to do a dance with his partner. I watched him dance and he was very good, but he wasn't anywhere near John. Then someone elbowed me and said, "You know, that guy's deaf."

When I went back and decided to write a new dance movie, I started from that moment. *Love N' Dancing* opens in 2002, when my character, Jake Mitchell, wins the world championship, but doesn't really feel he deserves it. Flash to the present day: Jake teaches dancing and does motivational speaking for kids (I always include something personal). It's at one of these school speeches where Jake meets Jessica (Amy Smart), a bored-with-life English teacher who has a workaholic fiancé (Billy Zane). Jake and Jessica ignite a flame in each other after Jessica becomes Jake's student, and they eventually compete for the world championship.

Right away, I had my assistant put together a list of the best dance films and romantic comedies. Then I went through and started to find email addresses and contact information for the directors of these films. (I'll explain this method in more detail in Chapter 12: The Attachment Approach.) I came upon a guy named Robert Iscove, who had directed the teen comedy *She's All That* (which made $150 million), and had even choreographed the movie *Jesus Christ Superstar* back in 1973.

I liked Rob right away, and he connected with the script. His notes were always well thought out and moved the story in a more positive direction. The only idea I resisted was to make the script focus more on the character's deafness. I didn't want to make it a "disability" story. As my friend Dr. Paul Stuart Wichansky (a fellow motivational speaker with cerebral palsy who served as the hearing loss consultant on *Love N' Dancing*) will tell you, it's better to see people for what they *can* do instead of what they *can't*. In *Love N' Dancing*, Jake's deafness is almost a side note. Our movie shows ability, not disability. Rob agreed with this approach, and we were ready to move.

As a producing partner, I chose Robert Royston, a legend in the swing dance community. He had over seven U.S. Open titles, and was the world champion in both swing and country dancing for four consecutive years. Robert is also a very charming individual and gives off an extremely positive vibe.

Robert was involved in *AnySwing Goes*. I had brought him in and introduced him to the SP, and Robert was hired to choreograph. After that film fell apart, Robert and I stayed close (he was also one of my first West Coast Swing teachers… I figured, why not learn from the best?). Together, Robert and I produced *The World Championships of Country Dance* for GAC TV in 2003. It was the first time competitive country dancing was ever broadcast, and it was very well received.

For *Love N' Dancing*, I knew that I needed Robert's full involvement, so I asked him to produce the film with me, and I wrote a nice supporting role for his wife, a theater actress who always wanted to make the transition to film.

The first dollar came in from an HNI dancer I knew from Long Island. I met with him and pitched him on the project, then invited him to a special screening of *The Attic*. This guy believed in the project and in me, so he gave me $25,000. It wasn't much, but it was a start. Through some family connections, Robert was able to find someone who wanted to invest another $25,000. Now we had $50,000 to develop our $3 million film.

Robert had a fantastic reputation in the swing dance world, and knew a lot of people with money. One was a world champion poker player. Robert and I met with him and pitched him on the project, but he was already sold. He was such a fan of West Coast Swing (being a dancer himself) that he had no doubt a movie featuring the dance would be a hit. This was potentially the easiest money that I've ever been involved in landing. The HNI poker player wired $500,000, no questions asked.

We were able to get a few more little hits, and we had around $700,000 when we started making offers for the lead role of Jessica. We focused on actresses who had prior dance experience. The bonus was that whomever we cast would get eight weeks of dance training with Robert Royston. We began getting bites right away.

It was a total surprise when we heard Amy Smart had dance training. I was a fan of *The Butterfly Effect* and *Road Trip*, and I thought she fit the character very well. We made the offer, and she accepted.

We had to make a "pay-or-play deal" (see Chapter 12: The Attachment Approach) with Amy, so we locked ourselves into a date. We had the money to pay her, but didn't have much more than that. We moved forward using the Dangerous Approach (see Chapter 13: The Dangerous Approach), which, though effective, is not highly recommended.

The reason we moved forward was because we had a major investment group in New York interested in funding the film. In fact, they committed verbally several times, and were one step away from committing on paper.

The problem was, being the star of the film, I could not focus even the tiniest bit of my efforts on raising money once the production started, or it would be seen all over my performance. I believe this is 100% necessary if you are an actor in your project. You cannot produce and act at the same time. It's just too much. I've heard of actors succeeding as they directed themselves (Clint Eastwood is a great example), but being a producer on set and starring in the movie is a recipe for disaster.

So I gave over the financing reins to Robert Royston and his sister-in-law, Melissa McDonald, along with her business partner, Beth Fisher. They all worked together raising money for the film. They were green, but they were effective because they were motivated. They learned the ropes quickly.

We hired Sylvia Caminer, a New York indie producer, to work as the nuts-and-bolts, experienced producer on set.

I don't know exactly what went on during production because, for better or for worse, I was kept out of it. Eventually, I believe, the New York group committed in writing, but the money never dropped. We got to a situation where we were almost done shooting, and our funds had run out. In the meantime, however, the team of Robert, Melissa, and Beth had raised somewhere in the realm of $1 million, which kept us going. We still needed that extra $2 million or so to finish, and we found out after shooting that we weren't getting it.

I returned home to Los Angeles, and the "crack high" of production ended instantly. We were faced with past due bills, vendors and crew that needed to be paid, and no money in our account. All the credit cards were maxxed out, and we were stuck.

Three lessons here:

◊ Never hand over the reins entirely. In fact, I got some flack from this during production when I found out my producing partner thought I wasn't doing enough. He took full credit for bringing the New York group, which leads me to my next lesson....

◊ Never take credit for bringing anyone or anything to the table until they have closed. I've actually seen this happen on several occasions, and each time it has blown up in the person's face.

◇ You can't sue anybody. What were we supposed to do when the New York group backed out? Sue them? They were a billion-dollar entity… we were broke. And say we did have the money to sue, what then? We would have ended up in a three-year lawsuit and the film would have crumbled and fallen long before then. Unfortunately, that's why filmmakers are such easy targets for scam artists. Scammers know that filmmakers are desperate, and they also know they won't sue.

We had shot the film in New Mexico, and when we were late paying people, they started getting really pissed. The most anger came from unpaid extras who were due something like $120. They thought we (as producers) were keeping the money hidden somewhere, or maybe spending it on luxury items. I racked up over $60,000 in credit card debt trying to live (the film owed me over $50,000 and it took eleven months to see that), and Robert actually got his electricity turned off in his house at one point.

Eventually, through some networking connections, I was introduced to Michael Roban, a great guy who runs Cold Fusion Media. Thankfully, Rob Iscove had started to cut the film for free with a great editor named Casey Rohrs. They had put together a "dog and pony show," and I showed that to Michael and his investors. I'm skipping over the running around, the sweating, and the endless happy pitches I gave so I can get to this: Cold Fusion came in, paid off the debt and saved the film. This wasn't a straight investment, however. It was "finishing funds," which I will explain in Chapter 14: The Structured Approach.

It still took us months and months to get everything straightened out. I can't tell you how many people threatened to sue Robert and me. If any cases against us had moved forward, the project would have simply collapsed, because we had $0.

You can't get blood from a stone. Throughout it all, Robert and I had only the best intentions, and why would we not? I knew I had the lead role, and that this could be a huge hit for me. As for Robert, his choreography would be on display for the whole film, and he's the producer.

When we finally screened the film in March 2008, we were ready for the hell ride to end. We'd find out soon enough, the road was just beginning to get bumpy. Basically, the film was very well received, and tons of video offers came in. We wanted a theatrical release. Two small theatrical offers came in, but they were nothing to write home about.

We soon realized that we needed to raise the P&A (prints and advertising) money ourselves and get the film into theaters. We went to our sales agents and said, "Go back to the distributors who are interested and ask them what they would do if we were bringing $3 million to the table."

Again, a classic example of "He who has the gold makes the rules." Distributors were suddenly all over us to help with the theatrical release for *Love N' Dancing*. We eventually chose a great group called Screen Media Films. Universal Home Video would be doing the video release.

Sounds simple, right? Wrong! We now needed $3 million! On top of that, we needed to pay off Cold Fusion's loan and a few other bridge loans, so we had to get our hands on nearly $5 million to get out of debt and release the film.

The fiascos that took place could merit their own book. Robert, Andy Goldstein (one of our executive producers), and I were at work fulltime for over six months trying to find an investor or lender to cover this gap. With our film growing older and everyone pushed to the edge, we finally accomplished our seemingly impossible goal. (This story is conveyed in Chapter 16: Getting It Done.) Robert and I continually joke about how good the book on *Love N' Dancing* will be, and I think we're holding off because the final act has not been written. I really hope the film is a success, because then it will all be worth it. But the gray hairs, the mental stress, and the internal damage done to us will always linger. Still want to be a film producer?

Status of the Market

Things have changed. Yes, the market for independent films is not that good right now, which will make it tougher for you to raise money. Don't fret, though. If you follow the methods in this book, I still believe you can get it done. The main thing I'm seeing from all investors (due to the faltering economy) is that they are all risk averse. You can counter that predisposition with formulas, utilizing tax rebates and tax write-offs, as well as foreign sales, which help or eliminate risk for investors. You'll find an in-depth discussion of this topic in Chapter 14: The Structured Approach.

Many great films are not getting distribution. No distributor wants to take the risk anymore. They are scared to put $20 million in P&A behind a film. Risk aversion has all but destroyed the market for indies. Years ago, you could make a great film (which is a feat in itself), then take it to a major festival, get a big money pickup, and see that film released into theaters. That's not happening anymore. The films that cost $8 million are being picked up for under $1 million (if they're lucky). It's very tough to make money on films that cost over $5 million unless you have a major star who can sell your project, and that list of potential candidates is getting smaller and smaller. Obviously, it's very tough to get a true *major* star behind your project. The most recent Demi Moore-Michael Caine movie went straight to video. She used to be one of the biggest stars in the world. Does that tell you something?

Years ago, a commercial film like *Love N' Dancing* would have been a layup to sell. In today's climate, we had to find a way to do it ourselves.

The Future

The future is uncertain. The Internet will be a force, but no one seems to be able to predict how it will be used, and very few (or none) seem to be able to find the formula to make money off of it.

But selling is not your top priority, though it is important. If you make money for your investors, you'll be able to line them up and get them to participate in future projects. If you make a ton of money, you're not going to need private equity, because you'll probably end up working for a studio. If you don't make money, you're going to have to find new investors (and explain why your last project didn't turn a profit).

This book deals with funding your film. Film sales are a different story. As a producer, it's your responsibility to set up a film to succeed financially as best you can. But film investment is a risk. Even people who invest in film all the time will tell you that. You need to keep this in mind as you look for investors. You will try like hell to make them money, but, at the end of the day, it's all a gamble. This book will deal with how to get those people to take a gamble.

When I refer to "those people," I'm talking about HNIs. HNIs are the folks everyone is after. They're not the ones who know the people (though they can be valuable too). They are the check writers. As I'll discuss in Chapter 10: The Finder's Fee Approach, the HNIs are not producers, and many of them are not even related to the film business at all. They have become successful in other industries and possess the financial resources to fund your movie. These are the people to target.

Your HNI network needs to be protected. I've had people "encroach" on my HNIs numerous times. It's part of the business of swimming with sharks. A way around this is to have producing partners sign a non-circumvent agreement, which states that they cannot approach your HNI for their projects. I highly encourage you to have a boilerplate version of this contract on your computer, and to hand it out to anyone who's talking to your investor. Getting an HNI is incredibly tough. The last thing you want is to put in tons of work gaining an HNI's interest in your film, and then watch as another producer swoops in and grabs that investor's money for his own project.

SIDE NOTE

Another way to combat this is to restrict yourself to high-level relationships. HNIs who are your good friends will let you know when someone with whom you're currently working approaches them.

Essentials

Before we start, there are some essentials we need to cover. These are tools you should have in your arsenal prior to beginning your efforts to start raising money.

IMDbPro

IMDbPro, the subscriber version of *IMDb*, has become a fixture in the film business. An invaluable online tool, it lists people's credits and contact information. Once you activate your account, you can do tons of research through this site's database. I run into people at festivals who frequently list their credits for me. I collect their business cards and, the next day, go right to IMDbPro. About 80% of the time, their credits aren't listed and I learn the person is full of it.

Always follow up with everyone you meet at a festival or at a networking event. If I had to attribute one thing to my success in financing films, it's the ability to follow up and stay persistent. Following up makes the difference between closing a sale and wishing you closed a sale.

With iPhones, Blackberries, and all other communication devices that come with built-in Internet access, you have access to IMDbPro right at your fingertips. Recently, I was trying to get into one of the hottest clubs in L.A. and I went to the front of the line. The bouncer asked if I was in the film business. I told him I was and rattled off a couple of credits. He pulled out his iPhone and IMDb'ed me right there, honest to God. I got in the club, so I guess my listing was okay.

I've also been on the opposite side, where I was doing the IMDb'ing. I was at an AFM (American Film Market) party and this guy told me he was a producer. His name sounded familiar, so as he was talking, I pulled out my Blackberry and IMDb'ed him, all the while pretending I was texting. Within a minute, I knew all of his credits and was able to use that to my advantage.

Remember to update yourself on IMDb. If you don't know how to do it, read the instructions or email the help desk. This is essential. The interface is not the easiest to use, and I'm saying this as a former computer guy. But you have to learn it because no one's going to update your listing for you. It's all about Starmeter if you're an actor, and it's all about credits if you're anything else. Whatever you are involved with, do the update yourself.

Variety or *Hollywood Reporter*

A subscription to one of these (or both) is more than essential. These periodicals are the lifeblood of the industry, the only publications that really cover and speak to our world. Years ago, I would read the articles in both and have no idea what they meant. Nowadays, I know or I am friendly with at least a few people in each daily edition.

I used to cut out pictures of studio executives or agents that appeared in the back of these magazines. That way, I could identify who these people were if I ran into them. It's your responsibility to know who the important people in your business are. This is your industry, and this will be how you make a living and perhaps support a family.

As you start to feel connected to the business, you'll realize why the trades are so crucial. You'll be able to use articles to your advantage. If you read in *Variety* that a friend just got promoted, make sure you call him or her and offer congratulations. If the *Hollywood Reporter* notes that 1234 Entertainment is buying scripts about trampolines, and you own the *Chinatown* of trampoline scripts, contact 1234 Entertainment. You'll find out quickly how to work the trades, the true glue of the industry.

Storymakers

This is the only TV show I know of that deals with the film business issues that true industry professionals care about. Hosted by Hollywood icons Peter Bart and Peter Guber, *Storymakers* (formerly known as *Sunday Morning Shootout*) on AMC is like a master class in producing. If you wish to be in the film business, watching the show is a requirement.

I wish that *Variety* would create its own cable channel one day, addressing the real business of film, with topics such as what spec scripts are selling and what financial deals have been made. Right now, all we have is E!, a channel most concerned with what Britney Spears was wearing when she left the airport, and whom Madonna was seen kissing.

For now, all the serious people have is *Storymakers*. Watch it religiously.

Computer Skills

Bottom line: If you haven't done so already, you need to gain computer proficiency. Most important, you must be able to email. This is kid's stuff. If you think you can be connected and not know how to send and receive email, you're very wrong.

I would also recommend getting a Blackberry, an iPhone, a Palm, or any phone that can send and receive instant email. I prefer the Blackberry because it's the only one with truly secure email capability at the moment.

Hundreds of emails go in and out of my account each day. It's just part of the business. You also need to be ready to bang the phones at all times, so get a good plan with a lot of minutes, and get a Bluetooth headset for your car.

In addition to emailing, you need to learn how to use database programs such as Microsoft Excel, and word processing programs like Microsoft Word. Both are vital. We'll explore these crucial tools more fully in later chapters.

Business Cards

Your presentation is so important. As you build your network, you'll start to give out and collect business cards on a daily basis. I have thousands. I can assure you, though, I've followed up with 90% of them.

VistaPrint is an Internet company that offers free business cards. All you have to do is pay the shipping and handling, which is under $5. The cards come with the VistaPrint logo on the back. If you think I'm giving you a tip here, think again. The second someone hands me a business card and I flip it over and see the VistaPrint logo, I know that person is full of shit.

Think about it. Say I'm talking to a guy who claims he's Mr. Producer. He's telling me he's got all kinds of projects in development. Okay, sounds great. But that VistaPrint logo indicates he can't afford to spend more than $5 on his business cards. Based on this information alone, I'll be quick to call his bluff.

The same goes for flimsy cards made from paper you bought at Staples. Do you really want this to be the first impression you make on potential collaborators or investors?

I'll even go further and say I don't even like cards that have been designed with template graphics on the Internet! I have a big problem with knowing that someone else might be out there with a business card that has the exact same design.

The only alternative is to have a business card, and perhaps your company logo, custom designed. There are companies on the Net that do this for $99. It's worth it. You are branding your company, and you are taking a step toward creating a unique image to match your unique voice.

You can also get creative here. My latest business card design uses movie posters from classic films. The backs of the cards all have the same contact information, but the front may feature the poster from *Double Indemnity*, *Casablanca*, or *The Third Man* (and I have tons more).

Don't cheap out on business cards. It can make you look bad from the start.

Website

I used to design websites and can make some great looking flash sites. If you have those skills, fantastic. If not, *don't design your own site!* The number of crappy websites I've seen rivals the amount of bad scripts I've read. Again, you may need to pay someone else to do this, but it is worth it. Check out some of my own websites:

◇ *www.trickcandle.com* (production company)

◇ *www.tommalloy.com* (acting)

◇ *www.howtosucceed.net* (motivational speaking)

◇ *www.bankrollthebook.com* (this book)

They are all professionally designed and represent me extremely well.

I'll convey a story about what a good website can do:

I designed the *trickcandle.com* site using some amazing template flash code from Blue Gel Media. I spent some money purchasing the code and graphics, and took about a week to design the site. I also optimized it for a Google search (a lot of web design companies will do this for you). Again, I used to do web design and I've been around computers my whole life, so I have an advantage. But let's say I spent $3000 on the site.

About a month after I went live with the site, I got a call from the production company of an actress who has won several Academy Awards. They saw my site and wanted to meet me. I went in and had a great discussion, and we're still trying to find a script of mine that's right for them to produce. Thanks to the inroads my website made for me, I now have this company as, at the very least, a contact.

Do you think they would have contacted me based on a simple HTML site that listed my credits? Never. They saw my site, thought that it was topnotch, figured I was a professional (which I am), and called me in. That's what a good website can do for you. Just like the business cards, you can't cheap out on this.

I've seen many people continue to design their own sites and think they look good. Maybe, like bad screenwriters, they just have no idea what works. Try attacking the website question the same way you would a script you've just written (I'll go over this in Chapter 4: Selling Yourself on the Project). Send the link out to random people who won't be afraid to be honest with you and get their opinions.

Finally

Welcome to Indiewood. Okay, so Indiewood is not the prettiest place in town, but, if you can become successful, you're sure to get a lot of respect. You must have a burning drive and passion coupled with non-stop persistence and focus. You also need to be in it for the long haul. It's going to be a roller-coaster ride. Hang on.

WHY YOU NEED
THIS BOOK

2

What Do You Have?

You may know people. You may have friends who are actors. You may have friends who are storyboard artists, experienced DPs, ADs, or line producers. You may even have a connection with a prestigious film producer. You also may have a killer script (more on that in Chapter 4: Selling Yourself on the Project). You may have free location, free equipment... even free film.

But you still need money.

At the end of the day, all that matters is "getting the gold." The golden rule of Hollywood is "He who has the gold makes the rules." I heard that expression a few years ago and have come to realize that there's nothing truer in the film business. To make your dream of a film a reality, you need money.

The Other Books

Over the course of my life, I've run into several books that promised to reveal the tricks and trades used to "finance your film." The one thing these books had in common was that when it came to the nitty-gritty, they all failed me.

Sure, the books would tell you how other people have done it, describing "negative pickup deals," and "bank financing," but I kept thinking, "How do *I* do that?" It's not easy for a filmmaker to just walk into Sony and say, "Hey, can I get a negative pickup deal for my film?" The funny thing is, if you're at all familiar with negative pickup deals, you'd know that you still need financing even if you have one!

I kept searching, hoping one of these books would reveal the true secret as to where to get the money and whom to get it from. So many of the books, including one whose entire focus is to show the reader how to write a perfect business plan, consigned the most important elements — the *how* and the *where* — to the filmmaker. I was dumbfounded. I had my perfect business plan, so now what? I had stories of how Kevin Smith got his film made (by maxing out his credit cards), so now what? Is that what you want me to do? Is that the only way to make a film?

I equate this lack of knowledge to two potential problems:

◊ Most of the people writing the other books have never funded a film. They were perhaps lawyers involved with drafting the documents for funding, or they schooled themselves in every aspect of how films are funded traditionally, but they themselves never went out and raised money for a film.

Or…

◊ They didn't want to truly give their secrets away. Let me explain:

People in the film business consider money a commodity. If I'm telling you that, at the end of the day, money is all that matters to a film, do you think that a person who knows where cash can be found will just give away that source? Hell no!

People with HNIs end up protecting them like a mother lion would protect her cubs. I'm guilty of it as well, and I make no excuses for it. I've gotten into screaming matches with people who tried to contact my HNIs behind my back. I've caught people trying to steal my investors red-handed. The HNI funds the projects that feed my wife and kids and pay for my house. Why wouldn't I want to protect that person?

I've already mentioned non-circumvent agreements and high-level relationships. Producers cling to their money people just like successful salesmen cling to their top clients. What amazes me is that, in other businesses, if you stole someone's client, you'd be thought of as a horrible person. If you steal someone's client or money person in the film business, you'd be considered nothing short of normal. It happens all the time.

The Most Important Thing to Learn

The single best thing you can do to raise money for a film is:

Stay away from anyone *who is associated with the film business.*

I once heard an entertainment attorney from Chicago put it best: "You want money for films, get outta Dodge!"

Now let me tell you why. Since I'm now considered very skilled at raising money for films, I get pitches coming to me all the time. People ask me, "Can you raise $3 million for my film?" Let's forget, for a moment, the merits of their projects, or any other aspects of their films. Let's just say I had an HMI who wanted to invest $3 million. Do you really think I would give him to someone else? Of course not! I would get him or her to give me the $3 million!

This lesson took me so long to realize. Trust me, I was on the other end for so long. I would pitch people in the film business all the time, hoping to raise money. While some enjoy funding other projects and don't want to be involved creatively at all, very few don't have their own agenda. The only exception is the producer who happens to be looking for the exact type of project you're developing. For example, say you have a romantic comedy, and that's what their financier also wants — but the producers only have a dramatic piece at the ready. This scenario is the exception to the rule; the majority of people in this business are only out to help their own projects.

While at the AFM in Santa Monica a few years ago (more on the AFM in Chapter 11: The Distributor Approach), I was in a lunch meeting with a guy I was approaching for funding for *Love N' Dancing*. As I was discussing what we needed budgetwise, I noticed he was half-listening. I threw out the name of an actress we were considering for the lead role. I'm not going to say who it was exactly, but let's pick a famous movie star: Charlize Theron. I said we were considering making an offer to Charlize, and his eyes lit up. Suddenly he had come to life! He turned to me and said, "Hey, I have a project that's perfect for her... do you think you can get her the script?" In that one second, I realized that this guy, even if he had money connections, would always put our film in second position. He was going to worry about his films first.

I've heard it happen dozens of times. Another financier friend of mine conveyed a story about meeting with some Wall Street investor types to pitch a slate of projects. In the middle of the meeting, the Wall Streeters asked him, "Well, what if we had our own scripts? Do you have ways to finance those?" Here was my friend, in a meeting with people he thought were investors, and they were picking his brain about how he operated, and eventually were asking him for financing!

Another friend (and this is one of my all-time favorite funding stories) had, on his own, raised $500,000 for a $1 million film. He started going out to potential financiers in the film business to see if he could raise the other 50%. His pitch was that he had the film half-financed, and he only needed the remainder. Well, he started putting out calls, and the people he called put out calls, and so on, until a few calls came back in. One investor claimed he could put up 50%. My friend thought that was great, until he realized the so-called investor was talking about the 50% that my friend had already brought to the table. He was pitching my friend with his own money!

36

People in Hollywood are only concerned with their own careers, and I don't blame them. The film business is *incredibly* tough. If successful people in the industry don't want to help you, it's not necessarily because they're bad. They are more than likely just trying to help themselves.

About ten years ago, a friend of the family won the Academy Award for Best Original Screenplay. He was the hot writer at the time (and still is), and he wanted to take a shot at directing. So the studios gave him a low-budget (by studio standards) film to direct, that came in at about $15 million. The film, unfortunately, bombed. I was actually a big fan of his directing effort, so, after a few years, I approached him to helm *The Alphabet Killer*. He emailed me explaining that he couldn't get a job directing in this town if he tried and that he would only be an albatross and an obstacle if I attached him to my script.

My friend had won an *Oscar*! He was on top of the world, right? Wrong. His Oscar and $1.95 could buy him a cup of coffee at the local deli, as far as directing goes. (Writing-wise, though, he makes millions, so don't feel too bad for him.) That's how quickly this business forgets you, writes you off, or tosses you to the side. Now, knowing that, can't you see why people only want to help themselves? They have to pay mortgages, rent, and buy food for their kids! Even if you were to offer them generous finder's fees, it's not going to help their careers. So using someone in the industry to try to fund your film is a mistake. You must remember that, whoever your industry friends are, they are looking out for themselves first and foremost.

Who Has Funded My Films?

Where have I raised my private equity money? Well, the most significant sources were a commercial furniture salesman from New Jersey; a Webmaster from upstate New York; a professional poker player from Las Vegas; a marketing guru from Arizona; and a guy from upstate New York whose uncle was on the Forbes 400 list. None had anything remotely to do with the film business, except that they all loved watching movies.

People outside the film industry want in. They want to have stars' cell phone numbers so they can call them as friends and say hello. They want to go out drinking with a movie star they idolized in the past. They want to be "in the club." Successful people in Hollywood are already in the club, so pitching them your film is only another way of asking them to help you gain admission. All the while, they're trying to retain their own membership.

Keep in mind that by pitching a person outside the industry, you are offering him or her a way in. I make sure my film investors get what they want. All five of the people I just mentioned are now producing multiple projects. And all four have movie stars' cell numbers programmed into their phones, due to my "letting them in."

This Book

This book will tell you how to take that idea that's festering in your head and turn your dream a reality. It is my intention to take you through the steps that are the most important to getting your film financed. I will not keep any secrets. I will divulge all I know about where, when, and how to find the money. If you follow the steps, I know you will be successful.

WHAT NO ONE ELSE CAN DO

3

How Valuable Are You?

Understand this: If you can raise money for a feature film, you have just separated yourself from 99% of independent film producers working today. That's how valuable you are.

Photo by Scott Sloan

The Attic's *Elisabeth Moss, Catherine Mary Stewart, and me in a calm scene before the storm.*

After I made *The Attic* come to fruition, I was allowed into an exclusive club called The Circuit, a group of the most successful people working in independent film in New York City. The Circuit contained producers, writers, and directors. Actors and actresses were banned (I guess no one wanted them showing up asking for jobs).

It was a really good idea thought up by a great guy named Mark Grande, who was, at the time, the head of Howard Stern's production company.

The Circuit's goal was to meet once a month and network with other successful people in Indiewood.

I was so excited at first to be meeting all these people. Some were directors who had done multiple projects. Some were producers who had over a dozen films under their belt. I soon found out, though, that all of them had one thing in common: They all wanted money. I also discovered something else: None of them had any idea how to get it.

Now, please don't take this the wrong way; I still think The Circuit was (and is) a great way to network, and if you have enough credits and clout to get in, go for it. (I've included their information at the end of the book.) Also, I haven't been to a meeting in years because I moved to Los Angeles, so I cannot attest to who attends nowadays. I just want to note that when I was going to meetings, I spoke with successful Indiewood people, and they still were all searching for the gold. Even the top people can't find it!

At the time, I had only raised financing for one feature film, *The Attic*, but there were still people in The Circuit very much interested in me because I had done What No One Else Can Do. My producer friend Isen Robbins put it this way: "Tom, you've become the pretty girl who everyone wants to take to the prom!" This is how valuable and important being able to finance films is in Indiewood.

Another story: I had written an action script that was passed on through some connections to a pair of very experienced producers. When I say "very experienced," I mean that they had both produced some of the most successful films of all time. They read my actioner, and they called me in for a meeting. Turns out that my violent action thriller (the first one I had written) didn't meet their criteria. In fact, the thriller was so violent and quirky, that it will most likely never get made, but it has helped me immensely because the writing is some of the best I've ever done.

These two producers told me how much they admired my writing skill and would love to find a way to work together. I would have been elated, except for the fact that the company they worked for, one of the monster mini-majors, had recently closed up shop. They couldn't pay me anything, but they did tell me that they were looking to put together $100 million for a film fund and might have it completed by the end of the year.

Then, following a little awkward pause, they turned to me and asked, "So, Tom, how did you finance all of your films?" I was flabbergasted. These gigantic producers were asking little ol' me for advice. Trust me, if I gave you the list of credits between these two, your jaw would hit the floor. The problem was, they were always used to having studio money at their disposal, and now, facing the independent route, they were searching for any advice they could find. Amazing. I still have the utmost respect for them and am still hoping they can get their financing so we can work together.

Again, it just goes to show you that if you can get the gold, you become a rare and invaluable commodity.

What Everyone Will Tell You

Now here's the problem. This is something you should watch out for: A lot of people will tell you they can raise money for films. Almost all of them are full of it. It took me a long time to learn how to qualify money people, and, in this chapter, I will impart all the techniques I know.

The first thing I will tell you is that you have to take the same steps with *everyone* — *no exceptions.* I don't care what the potential financier looks like, or what he or she is wearing, or where you are meeting him or her. While 99% of these people you take the steps with will go nowhere, that final 1% will make your dream come true!

I learned this lesson the hard way. I was at a Christmas party at a celebrity friend's house, and my wife, who's so charming and friendly that she actually doubles my pitching powers just by being by my side at parties, was talking to a casually dressed man wearing penny loafers. My wife tugged at my arm, "Tom, you should meet this guy. He finances films." It was the holiday season, I was having fun, and the last thing I wanted to do was talk business. On top of that, my celebrity friend had more celebrity friends coming over and I was excited to meet them. Also, I was just so sick of people telling me they "finance films" that I simply didn't feel like taking the proper steps. So, to make a long story short, I blew the guy off.

He turned out to be one of the people on the Forbes 400 list. He also founded one of the biggest Internet companies in the world (I won't mention the name, but let's just say it's part of all of our vocabularies now), and he had funded about ten films, three of which were nominated for Academy Awards. Ughh.

That little lesson served as a reminder to me to follow up with everyone! So I'm starting this part of the chapter with a warning: Always take the steps. If the person turns out to be a fake, call it practice for you and your pitch.

What To Watch Out For

The phrase that everyone in the film business uses to qualify an investor is "Is he or she real?" The word "real" is the ultimate assessment. I've gotten to the point where I have met so many people who just talk and promise and talk some more than I am skeptical of everyone. To me, potential investors aren't real until:

◊ They've invested in my films before.

Or...

◊ They are writing me a check.

Only then will I consider them *true* HNIs.

Honest to God. If someone calls me on the phone and says, "Tom, I promise that I'm gonna send you the check for $2 million tomorrow!" I give that about a 20% chance of coming to pass. I've had people tell me funds were going to "close" so many times, and I'd say it actually happens one out of every fifty times. So you have to have a healthy skepticism. Never put all your eggs in one basket (see Chapter 9: The Ten-Arm Approach).

Have They Invested in the Past?

The first thing to ask a potential investor is what his or her story is. It's a great way to start a pitch, too, because people really like to hear themselves talk. They also like to tell you their stories... it's cathartic, in a way. Now, if this investor has never financed a film before, a red flag should go up. And, if this investor has never invested in anything before, a *monster* red flag should go up! Neither means that he or she is a dead end, but the second question is probably the most important thing I can offer you: Has this person ever invested in anything? If investments have been made in the past, has it been in films? Which ones have the investor been involved with?

So many have been burned investing in independent film, it's actually easier to close someone who hasn't financed one in the past. But they key is, they have to have invested in something. You want the people who have money to get rid of and are hungry for a piece of the film business.

SIDE NOTE

There's a horrible joke associated with independent film. It goes:
Q: How do you make a small fortune in independent film?
A: Invest a large fortune.

I say this joke is horrible because if you share it with an investor, you're probably dead in the water. The truth is, most independent films are made as labors of love, without any ideas on marketing or selling the film in the long run. If you make a film about two gay college roommates in Oklahoma, it might be personal to you, but where's it going to play? Japan? France? Germany? Hell, it probably won't even play in Oklahoma! I'll get more into marketing later (see Chapter 4: Selling Yourself on the Project), but understand that the stigma associated with independent films is that they don't make money. You need to be able to change that.

What Is Their Background?

It goes against everything I said in the beginning of this chapter, but part of the qualification process is looking at who the person is. For instance, one time I was invited to be introduced to a "financier." He showed up in a beat-up old convertible, wearing sweatpants and a sweatshirt. He was also missing some teeth. Now, he could have been an "eccentric millionaire," so I took all the initial steps, but I found out right away that this guy was just a wannabe. He actually said to me, "Look, the goal for all of us is to one day not have to work outside the film business." Turns out this guy had another full-time job. I said, "Well, I don't work outside of the film business," and he just stared at me. Can you guess what happened next? That's right… he started pitching me on two scripts that he had written.

Appearance definitely plays an important role here. Do you know where the person lives? There's a big difference between living in Beverly Hills and Reseda. There's a big difference between living on the Upper East Side of Manhattan and the South Bronx. Again, there are always exceptions to the rule, but I have found that simple things such as what the person is wearing, where he or she lives, and what he or she is driving do make a difference. One of my investors has about eight cars, including a Lamborghini, which he was driving the first day I met him. Right away I was able to make certain assumptions about him, including that he had enough money to buy a $250,000 car.

Another investor, who was visiting L.A. for only six days, had both his Lamborghini and his Ferrari flown in so he could drive them around town. That's right, he actually paid $9000 per car to have them by his side for his visit. Do you think this guy has some money to throw around?

Yet another had a gigantic loft in Manhattan. The thing had to cost him $6–7 million! Of course a guy like that needed a tax write-off, and, thanks to Section 181 of the Job Creations Act of 2004, film investment is a tax write off!

Los Angeles is all about image. I found that out quickly, because I moved into a house that was gigantic, and I didn't upgrade my car. I'm not really a car guy, so I kept driving my Chrysler Sebring because it was reliable and worked for me. What happened? Well, when I showed up at events, no one thought I was important. (You'd have to pull up in a BMW, Mercedes, Bentley, Aston Martin, Ferrari, or Maserati for that.)

But, when people visited my house, they thought I was rolling in it. Truthfully, I fit somewhere in between my car and my house. If someone was qualifying me and they came to my house, they would think I was a millionaire! If someone was qualifying me and I showed up at a Starbucks with my 2004 Sebring, they would think I was full of it. Either way they'd be wrong.

More often than not, your initial assumptions are true. If someone has to work another job outside the film business and considers himself "in the Industry," he's wrong. The only people who truly retain this status are those working in it full time. There's no middle ground for film. Actors and writers can get away with working in restaurants or bars, but producers have to be 100% committed. And the real actors and writers are working as actors and writers.

Never Pay a Fee

How do I know this? Yup, you guessed it. I learned this one the hard way too.

I met with a group out of New York City that was going to take my 15% equity (which I had raised myself) and structure financing to make it a full 100% budget. (Structuring can work. See Chapter 14: The Structured Approach.) Here was the catch: This company required a $60,000 "advisory fee." I can't be clearer about this: If anyone asks for an advisory fee or "consultant fee," run in the other direction! No one (and least who I know) legit takes any upfront fees. Fees are given out once the financing is achieved. And trust me, no one forgets about fees… in fact, you have to avoid the hundreds of people who will try to jump on your "money train" once your film is financed. But upfront fees do not exist in legitimate financing.

In the above-mentioned story, I ended up giving this group $60,000, and they did nothing for my film. We eventually dissolved the LLC, picked ourselves up, and started from the beginning. It was a horrible loss of financing. This company knew that we had so little money with which to sue them (remember the lesson about suing big companies), and since the legal process takes so much time, that we would just walk away. Which is exactly what we did. Lesson learned… the hard way.

Never pay any upfront fees! You want a consultant? This book is your consultant. You've paid a lot less than $60,000 for some hard-won advice.

Remember, qualify your HNI, and make sure he or she is real. Then move forward with all the techniques in this book. If and when you get a film financed successfully, you'll have already separated yourself from the pack by being able to achieve what no one else can.

SELLING YOURSELF ON THE PROJECT

4

Would You Invest?

What if you had $2 million liquid that could be invested? You worked hard for a long time and saved up that money. You have an income stream that supports your family, and you have a large mortgage payment. You'd really like to turn that $2 million into $3 million or $4 million. So what would it take for you to invest your money into someone else's project?

This is the initial qualification through which I run all of my own projects. If you had the money, of course you would finance your own project because it's yours and you love it! But that's not going to get you financed. Distance yourself from the project and pretend it's being presented to you. Ask the hard questions. Just suppose you had $2 million and your twin was walking into the room to pitch you on his or her film. Be as tough as you can be! This is your hard-earned money. You might have to imagine someone else in your position. Say, for instance, your parents are retired and have $500,000 saved up. That's all they have in the world. If you lost their money, they'd be on welfare. Would you feel confident pitching them on your project?

You have to take a hard look at the outcome. If you're pitching a project that's a dramatic piece with a touchy subject starring you (and you're not a name), written by you (and you've never written a script before and you're not WGA), and directed by you (and you've never directed a script before and aren't in the DGA), do you really think it's likely to be profitable if you make it for $5 million?

My favorite story about blue-skying an investment happened when I met this guy named John. He had a war movie that he wanted to direct. The budget: $100 million. Only the script hadn't been written yet. He was asking me about financing, not realizing that my niche is the $1 million – $8 million range (I can't think of that many $100 million independents). John had not only never directed a feature, he'd never even directed a commercial. I asked him what actors he saw in the lead roles. He said that he wanted to cast all unknowns. I'm sure you're thinking this is a joke, but it's not. John actually wanted someone to invest $100 million into his film with no script, directed by an unknown and inexperienced director, and featuring a cast of nobodies. Needless to say, John's war movie is still in the "development" stage.

I've seen it at lesser levels. I met with a woman who wanted her dramatic film to be made. "The script is pretty good," she said. (Yeah, "pretty good" is going to make someone jump for joy and throw money at her.) I asked her what the budget was and she said, "$5 million to $7 million." I asked her how many locations she had and she said, "It takes place in one house." I asked her whom she saw in the lead role and she said simply, "I'm playing the lead."

Okay, folks, if you had $5 million, and it was all you had saved up in your life, would you give it to her? I don't even think she would give it to herself!

But what if I told you this: I have a project that's going to cost you $2 million. It's a scary movie, which is a sellable genre, and it's directed by John Smith (fictional name, but let's say his last film grossed $60 million), and Johnny Star is already attached to play the lead (again, fictional, but let's just say he's a bankable name). We also have foreign sales estimates from 123

Pictures (a fictional-yet-reputable company) of $2 million on the lowest end, and a 35% New York City tax credit, which amounts to over $700,000 back when the film is finished. On top of that, the script is amazing, and will attract enormous talent in the supporting roles because of Johnny Star and John Smith. My guess is that I can triple an investor's money within a year and a half.

Would you invest in that one? I would! If all those elements were true, who wouldn't? Be careful, though. Pay attention to what I just said. All those components need to be accurate. Is Johnny Star *really* attached? I can tell you I've seen this about a hundred times. A producer says that they have Mr. or Mrs. Star attached, and when it comes down to the nitty-gritty, that star isn't connected to the picture in any way. Make sure you have it on paper.

Another one of my favorites is the director who claims he can bring a star to the project because he or she is "one of my best friends." Don't fall for this. I've experienced this several times, and each promise fell through. I have a lot of great friends. Does that mean I would risk my career and my living to help them out in a project? No. Think about that when this director is telling you that his "celebrity friend" will surely "jump on board." Only believe it when it's on paper.

For the purposes of this exercise, let's say every part of the John Smith-helmed scenario I described above was true. If so, it would be a lock to make money for your investors. Instead of asking them for money, what would you be doing? You'd be giving them a gift! If you could guarantee someone you could triple his or her investment, you'd want to give this opportunity to all your friends and family, right?

And that's how I approach a film investment. It's a gift that I am giving. You must do the same — view your film as an investment that will transform itself into a gift. Yes, you are asking for money, but you will be giving back more value than you are requesting. That's the key. (More on this in Chapter 10: The Finder's Fee Approach.)

Step 1: The Amazing Script

Before I started writing, I took it upon myself to read all the screenplays from great and classic films that I could find. I would suggest this approach to anyone. The scripts I started reading all worked. Unfortunately, that has soured me for almost every screenplay that followed. I have probably read about 600 screenplays in my life (not counting those classics), and I've hated around 580 of them. It's not that I go in wanting to hate them… just the opposite. I start on the first page hoping it will blow me away. But, 90% of the time (or more), I'm let down.

Why is this? Well, first off, everyone believes he or she can write. Directors, actors, janitors, bartenders, fishermen, teachers… everyone! I just don't see why that is. Does everyone believe he or she can be an eye surgeon? Or a car mechanic? No. But writing's a different story. That's why the WGA has to retain such strict standards for admission.

I've had horrible scripts given to me by actors who are famous or have been in the business for twenty years. Remember the WBD I mentioned earlier (who was also an editor)? Well, he gave me a script that was literally unreadable, and this guy had edited some gigantic features, one of which made $300 million.

The most important lesson for independent films is this: *The script is king.*

You want to make an independent film? You cannot start with an okay script. You cannot start with a good script. You have to start with a fantastic script! That's the only way I can say you've safely hedged your bets to get your film made.

How do you know if you have a great script? Have multiple people who know what they're talking about read it. One approach is to go to *www.Craigslist.com* and click on the Los Angeles version. Place an ad for script readers. You will receive tons of great resumes from people who have been script readers for major studios. You can get a few of these people to read your script and give you studio-level coverage for $60-$100. Don't put your name on the script. Doing so might lead the reader to censor his or her comments.

The reason you're having multiple people read your script (at least three) is that you want to look for trends. Readers, even the experienced ones, have likes and dislikes. Or they misinterpret things. In coverage for a dramatic piece I wrote, the reader assumed the main character killed a man about twenty pages into the story (when, in actuality, he just beat the guy up). This plot point was clear to everyone who read the script but her, and it soured her whole coverage. She went forward saying, "The lead character shows no remorse throughout the entire script!" Obviously, she didn't get it, and that can happen. To fight this, have multiple people read your work and give you feedback. If everyone says, "The supporting characters need to be developed more," then that's what you should do.

Writing is rewriting. Even with the great script, you're going to be rewriting it seventeen times before it actually gets shot. Actor A might come to the set wanting to change dialogue. You might have to change a scene because you lost a location. You could need to write a quick "filler" scene at the last minute. All kinds of problems arise. So start thinking of your script (much like you're going to think of your business plan in the next chapter) as a living, changing organism.

So what if you can't write? You have to be honest with yourself about this issue. It won't necessarily stop your movie from getting made. There's a simple solution: Find someone who can write. Pay him or her to rewrite your script or option one of his or her scripts. There are great scripts out there... you just have to find them.

Search everywhere: IMDbPro, Craigslist, and your network. Approach your foreign sales agent contacts (we'll go over how to get those in later chapters) and ask them if they have scripts. You may even want to turn to managers and agents. Once you have a script, do the coverage test that I already explained. Good and more experienced readers will "pass" on just about everything you send them. That's what you want... a discerning eye.

Make sure you are only moving forward with a *killer* script. I can't stress how important this is. Great scripts find a way to get made.

Step 2: Think from a Marketing Mindset

Let's go back to the beginning of the chapter where I asked you to consider your project from an outsider's perspective. Would you invest your life savings? That's what you may be asking someone else to do.

Certain rules for marketing apply, but keep in mind that every rule has an exception. Generally, though:

◊ Genre films, on an independent level, are easier sells. These include action (never out of style), horror (though the market is always flooded with these), and martial arts (another form of action). As far as foreign sales go, all these genres sell. Domestic comedies usually don't. Urban films usually don't. Heavy dramatic pieces usually don't.

◊ Stars are what will get your project financed. Certain stars matter when it comes to foreign sales. You have to hook up with a reputable foreign sales agent and find out who these actors are. Some of these sales agents have given me lists specifying the dollar value of specific stars. (I'll go over this more in Chapter 11: The Distributor Approach)

◇ An experienced director helps with casting. If you were Jessica Hotshotstar, would you want to risk your career on an unknown, untested director? (I already conveyed a story to you about how quickly you can become history in this town.) That's why a lot of directors do short films or shoot their inaugural projects guerilla-style… so they have a calling card. An experienced director doesn't require this. On top of that, chances are that the experienced director knows some talent he or she can call and bring to the project.

◇ Pick a script (or write a script) that can be shot anywhere. Don't choose one that has to be shot in the Colorado Rockies (unless it is truly a killer script and must be shot in Colorado), because if you find an investor from Louisiana, he's probably going to want you to shoot the film in New Orleans. Almost all of my scripts that I have made into films are not "location contingent," which also allows us to pick states that offer tax incentives (more on this in Chapter 13: The Structured Approach).

◇ Don't go crazy with the amount of locations in the script. For a first film, it helps to set it in one location — I did this with *The Attic*. Do you have a scene in the script that calls for a shot in Yankee Stadium? Well, there goes at least $500,000 of your money, which will pay for the rental fee and the cost of filling the stadium with extras and cardboard cutouts.

It's crucial that you factor in and analyze all of the above before you move forward with your project.

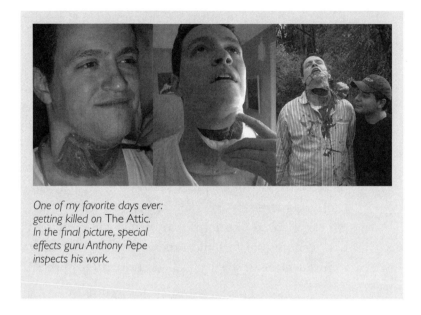

One of my favorite days ever: getting killed on The Attic. *In the final picture, special effects guru Anthony Pepe inspects his work.*

Step 3: Be Realistic!

Okay, maybe you wrote a script so you could direct. Or perhaps you want to play the lead role (I've been there!). What do you do? Well, you have to be realistic and you accept that you have just set up roadblocks or "financial liabilities" to getting your film financed.

The exception to this is if you are a proven director or a marketable star. But even those examples carry restrictions. If you're a proven director in the horror genre, your name attached to a comedy isn't going to mean much. The same goes for an actor or actress trying to cross genres or media.

I had an actress friend who was a comedy TV star. When I told her I was looking for attachments for an indie drama, she asked me to consider her. I think she got insulted when I told her it would be a tough sell. She said to a mutual friend, "What, he doesn't think I'm famous enough?" The fact is, any fame she had from the comedy world would actually hinder my little drama. It would be better if she were an unknown. That's why comedy stars have such a tough time making the transition to drama. People see their faces, remember the work they've done, and want to laugh.

The bottom line here is that even if you do have a little cachet, you have to factor in what you may or may not bring to the project.

You must consider your liabilities — anything that would stand in the way of getting your financing. Remember, you can get around any obstacle if you just be realistic.

Let's say you have a script that takes place in one house (this is good) and you're playing the lead role (and let's assume you're not a big star, so that's liability #1). Instead of attaching a well-known, established director, you want your film school buddy to direct his first feature (liability #2). The budget for your film is $5 million (insanity #1).

The scenario above emphasizes the difference between liability and insanity. Liabilities can be dealt with. Insanity cannot.

If you really wanted to make the above-mentioned movie, why not try to shoot it for $400,000? With technology and the lack of professional projects out there (you'll find out very quickly that if you can get your films funded, you're likely to be the only game in town), and the one location, it can be done. You can make a professional movie for $300,000. I made *The Attic* for $500,000 and got the director of *Pet Sematary* to direct it. Wanting your friend from film school to direct your project is okay; it's just a liability. So drop the budget. Again, though, script rules all! If the script is good (and it has to be, even for $400,000), you may be able to eke out a little more.

Another example: Say you have a horror film (bonus), and you have three major roles all available for stars (bonus), but you want to direct the film and you're a first-time director (liability).

Okay, that project is not too bad, especially if the script is killer. It could be fundable if the budget is not too high.

As an actor, I'm a liability in the lead role, because I am not a big star (yet). So how did I handle this? I wrote *The Attic* and *The Alphabet Killer* with strong female leads and an ensemble cast around them. I played the third biggest role in each film, and was able to surround myself with stars whose names would help market and fund the film. For *Love N' Dancing*, I trained in West Coast Swing for over eight years so I "job secured" myself into the role. As I said earlier, my pitch was, "You can cast Matt Damon, but he can't dance like I can!" And it was still incredibly tough! Liabilities are not insurmountable, but they sure add headaches. Try to limit these as much as possible. If you are starring in the film, hire an established director. If you are directing the film, hire stars. And if you have neither, drop the budget.

A Final Word

A final word on selling your project to yourself: Being realistic is very tough but essential. You are already sold on your own project. Forget the fact that it's your baby, and you know in your heart it will make money. Trust me, I've been there. But if you can truly step back and ask yourself, "Would I put money into this if I wasn't involved?" and the answer is (as much as it hurts) "No," then you need to rethink your project.

You must get to the point where you would invest your own money into the movie in a heartbeat if you had it. You would have your parents give away their life savings. You would spend your kids' college fund on it… anything! You'd do this because you know you will be getting the money back!

Then, and only then, when you're that confident, will you be ready to proceed.

CREATING THE
BUSINESS PLANS

5

Note the Plural

You're not going to create one business plan. You're going to create many. Not that they will be much different from each other. They will all follow the same general format. You may have more success shifting around aspects of the plan and redesigning certain areas. There's no room for mediocre presentations in the film financing business.

You're not going to create an okay business or a good business plan or even a very good business plan. You're going to create a killer business plan.

So many people make the same mistake. Their business plans are under-researched, under-designed, and unprofessional. What's worse is that they create one business plan and stick with it. Yours has to be beautiful, convincing, and most of all dynamic. You have to be able to create multiple versions for multiple potential financiers. Some money people want to be sold on projections, some want to be sold on risk management, some want to be sold on sizzle. None will want the same generic business plan.

This is not a book on business plans. As I mentioned earlier, entire books are devoted to that subject. The format of the business plan I've included is my own and comes from a long period of trial and error. And it works. It has done its job for me in the past, and will hopefully do so in the future. I'm including it here.

While part of me believes I'm giving away the farm by revealing my proprietary stuff, I'll take solace in the fact that this is one aspect of my career I won't have to explain at those diner meetings anymore. So here is a general business plan for a non-existing film. It will explain each component and identify which parts will change, which will stay, and what will sell.

Confidential Information Overview

Just giving information here. Nothing binding.

Month, Year

Date it, and keep it current. Never give the business plan to anyone, unless this date reflects the current month.

Contact:

Tom Malloy
123.456.7890 (p)
tmalloy@bankrollthebook.com

Self-explanatory, but note that I've placed my actual email address from the book site here to share with you.

LEGAL DISCLAIMER

◊ This Confidential Information Overview (this "CIO") contains confidential information regarding TRICK CANDLE PRODUCTIONS (the "Company"). By accepting this CIO the recipient agrees that it will, and will cause its directors, officers, employees, advisors and other representatives to, use this CIO and any other information supplied by or on behalf of the Company only to evaluate a possible transaction with the Company (the "Transaction") and for no other purpose, will not divulge or permit others to divulge any such information to any other person and will not copy or reproduce in whole or in part this CIO. The recipient, by acceptance hereof, acknowledges its duty to comply with this certain Confidentiality Agreement between the recipient and the Company.

All of this information has been prepared for me by an attorney.

◊ The information contained in this CIO was obtained from the Company and other sources believed by the Company to be reliable. No assurance is given as to the accuracy or completeness of such information. This CIO does not purport to contain all the information that may be required or desired to evaluate the Company or the Transaction and any recipient hereof should conduct its own independent analysis of the Company and the data contained or referred to herein and the Transaction. In determining whether or not to proceed with a Transaction, the recipient must rely on their own examination of the Company and the Transaction.

◊ No person has been authorized to give any information or make any representation concerning the Company or the Transaction not contained in this CIO and, if given or made, such information or representation must not be relied upon as having been authorized by the Company. Statements in this CIO are made as of the date hereof. The delivery of this CIO at any time thereafter shall under any circumstances create an implication that the information contained herein is correct as of any time subsequent to the date hereof or that there has been no change in the business, condition (financial or otherwise), assets, operations, results of operations or prospects of the Company since the date hereof. The Company undertakes no obligation to update any of the information contained in this CIO, including any projections, estimates or forward looking statements.

◊ Any statement, estimate or projection as to events that may occur in the future (including, but not limited to, projections of revenue, expenses and net income) were not prepared with a view toward public disclosure or complying with any guidelines of the American Institute of Certified Public Accountants, any federal or state securities commission or any other guidelines regarding projected financial information. Such statements, projections and estimates are inherently imprecise and unreliable and the assumptions upon which they are based may prove to be incorrect. Achieving such statements, estimates or projections will depend substantially upon, among other things, the Company achieving its overall business objectives and other factors (including general, economic, financial and regulatory factors) over which the Company may have little or no control. There is no guarantee that any of these statements, estimates or projections will be attained. Actual results may vary significantly from the statements, estimates and projections, and such variations may be material and adverse.

◊ Recipients should not construe the contents of this CIO as legal, tax or investment advice. Recipients should consult their own competent counsel, accountant, tax, business and other advisors as to legal, accounting, tax, business and other matters concerning the Company or any Transaction. This CIO does not purport to be all-inclusive or to contain all the information that a recipient may require. Recipients are advised of the need to conduct their own thorough investigation of the Company and its industry.

TABLE OF CONTENTS

Self-explanatory. Nice and clean presentation.

Logo is repeated here. Just makes the page look nicer.

EXECUTIVE SUMMARY

Don't ever beat around the bush. State what you're looking for right away.

⟨⟩ **Trick Candle Productions** is seeking $3 million to complete the full production of the film *The Investigator* in 2009.

This first line is so important. I'll explain in more detail later in the chapter, but I place it up top because risk management is such a priority in these financial times.

⟨⟩ $3 million investment is backed by a **Risk Management Procedure** (see page 5), allowing for a possible risk of only 20 cents on the dollar.

They will be able to see this from the bios.

⟨⟩ **Experienced and Successful Production Team**

More risk management here. We're presenting distribution right away. It also shows that someone legitimate is interested in the film.

⟨⟩ **123 Pictures Foreign Sales** – One of the top foreign sales companies in the world has agreed to represent *The Investigator* in all foreign markets and has projected $1.2 million as minimum sales.

This is active at the time of this publication.

⟨⟩ **Independent Film Tax Credit** – US federal government has a tax write-off for independent film producers. (See Appendix D)

Explain to the investor right away how they are going to get their money paid back. I normally go with 25% off the top, then the typical 50/50 split between the production company and the investor.

⟨⟩ **Recoupment** – Investor will have priority in being reimbursed in an amount equal to one hundred and twenty five (125%) percent of his/her entire capital contribution to the Company. At that point, he/she will own 100% of the investor's side of the film for the life of the project. (See Appendix A)

RISK MANAGEMENT OVERVIEW

Here is a breakdown of how the risk of investing $3 million into this film is managed:

$3,000,000 – *The Investigator*

At the end of the two year period, if there is no profit, the following money is projected to be returned to the investor, even before a domestic sale!*:

⟨⟩ $1,200,000 in tax credits (40% credit from Michigan)

I'm picking Michigan here because it currently offers the largest tax incentive.

⟨⟩ $1,200,000 foreign sales projected from 123 Pictures (min. projection!)

Make sure you have this in writing. You are going off of the minumum projection from a reputable company.

TOTAL:	$2,400,000
RISK:	$.20/$1.00

Essentially, the HNI will only be risking $600,000.

In addition, "Accredited Investors" will be eligible for a 35% tax relief in accordance with section 181 of the American Jobs Creation Act, 2004 (see Appendix D). Adding that to the scenario should place the investor **beyond 100% coverage** on his/her investment, and this is not predicated on any domestic distribution!

Fantastic! You're telling the investor, on the second real page of the plan, that he or she is beyond covered. Think about it....Your HNI hasn't even learned what the project is about and you're already covering his or her investment.

* Note that these are worst-case scenario, minimum numbers. If the films make more than 20 cents on the dollar on a domestic sale, it will be profitable.

And right here you're letting them know how easy it is to start showing them profit and making them money.

PREVIOUS TOM MALLOY PRODUCED FILMS

You may not be able to supply this page, and that's okay. I am able to list past films that I produced. Notice that I'm not showing profit on them yet because all three were recently made. That's fine. Just make sure to attach legitimate projections.

The Attic (2006)

DVD Release Date: January 15, 2008
Director: Mary Lampert
Producers: Tom Malloy, Aimee Schoof, Isen Robbins, Russ Terlecki

Budget: $550,000.00

Cast: John Savage, Jason Lewis, Tom Malloy, Elisabeth Moss, Catherine Mary Stewart

Sales:
$125,000 Advance, New Films Intl, Foreign Sales
$75,000 Advance, Allumination Films, Domestic
DVD was released to all video outlets on January 15, 2008.
Sales projections are attached. (see Appendix D)

The Alphabet Killer (2007)

Still in POSTPRODUCTION
Director: Rob Schmidt (*Wrong Turn*)
Producers: Tom Malloy, Aimee Schoof, Isen Robbins, Russ Terlecki

Budget: $2,100,000.00

Sales:

Cast: Eliza Dushku, Cary Elwes, Tim Hutton, Tom Malloy, Michael Ironside

Still in POSTPRODUCTION
Foreign sales projections are attached. (See Appendix D)
Domestic deal with Anchor Bay, theatrical release in November, video release in February

Love N' Dancing (2007)

Still in POSTPRODUCTION
Director: Rob Iscove (*She's All That*)
Producers: Tom Malloy, Robert Royston, Sylvia Caminer

Budget: $5,700,000.00

Cast: Amy Smart, Billy Zane, Tom Malloy, Betty White, Caroline Rhea, Leila Arcieri, Rachel Dratch

Sales:

Still in POSTPRODUCTION
Foreign sales projections are attached. (See Appendix D)
Domestic deal currently being negotiated.

PROJECT SYNOPSIS

The Investigator is a dramatic crime thriller about Jason Harper, an ace detective with the Detroit Police Department.

When Jason is questioned about his drug use, he goes into a fury and quits the force. In the meantime, one of his cases is starting to make waves. A serial killer is striking victims, and Jason may be the only one who can put this guy away.

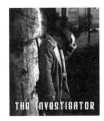

Self-explanatory. Make it sound good, though, because the HNI may not ever read the script.

Jason is forced to do the investigation from afar, as the New York Police Department wants nothing to do with him. But Jason may be the only chance future victims have. Can he conquer his personal demons before he's able to stop another?

BOX OFFICE & MARKETING / DISTRIBUTION

The Investigator, upon its completion, will be immediately shopped around to the major studios, including Universal, Paramount, The Weinstein Company, Lionsgate, Sony, and Warner Brothers. Producer Tom Malloy also has access to the acquisitions executives at all these studios.

Explained in more detail later in the chapter.

The primary goal of the Company's marketing efforts will be to achieve domestic theatrical release for the film, since this is the single most important determinant of a picture's performance in the subsequent markets of home video, cable and broadcast television, and foreign markets. *The Investigator* has the potential for a big sale because the budget is low and the script is excellent.

The Investigator
Crime Thriller, Indie Drama

Make sure to compare it to similar, successful films. The HNI is going to flip out when he or she sees the returns. But remember to tell them not to expect that kind of return.

Film	Budget	Worldwide Gross	ROI
Lost in Translation	$4,000,000	$119,723,856	2893.09%
Reservoir Dogs	$1,200,000	$2,832,029	136.00%
The Usual Suspects	$6,000,000	$23,341,568	289.02%
Memento	$9,000,000	$39,723,096	341.36%

PRODUCTION PLAN

This page is self-explanatory, and sometimes overlooked. More detail later in this chapter.

The following stages will begin upon capitalization of the film fund.

(a) **Packaging:** During this stage, the Company will "package" the film (i.e., attach actors, directors, key production personnel and other talent);

(b) **Preproduction:** During this period (the eight weeks prior to the start of production), the Company will open a production office; hire all crew; engage a locations scout to secure the locations where shooting will occur; secure rentals for camera and lighting packages; prepare shooting schedules; etc. At this time, all actors will be cast and finalized.

(c) **Production:** The production period (less than 30 days) will be the time that the principal photography will be shot. After this time, all of the scenes for the movie will be completed or "in the can"!

(d) **Postproduction:** During the postproduction period (approximately three to four months), the director and editor will select the best "takes" of the various scenes and edit those takes into an assembly of the entire film. Also, music will be acquired or composed, recorded and added to the film; an "optical" facility will create fades and dissolves between scenes, and shoot the "titles" sequences. The director may also do "looping sessions" (re-recording the actors' voices in a sound studio) and "Foley sessions" (creating sound effects).

TIMELINE

- Preproduction – **8 weeks**
- Production – **18 days**
- Postproduction – **3-4 months**
- Picture Lock (Total Time for Finished Product) – **6 months**
- Sellable film by **6 months**

Very important to the investor. When am I getting paid?

Goal: *The Investigator* is sold and profitable within 8 months from completion.

68

APPENDIX A

PROJECTED INVESTMENT RETURN

◇ First payout goes to investors until 125% of the investment is recouped.

◇ After 125% recoupment, the profit is split 50/50 between the investors and the production company. The 50% production company split consists of percentages given to the director, producers, actors, actresses, writer, etc.

◇ On the investment side, your individual investment reflects the percentage of the film you own, in this case 100% of the investor's side of the film for the life of the project.

The Investigator

Total Budget = $3,000,000

Sales of the Film = $5.5 million

First payout = $3,750,000

Remaining money to be split = $1.75 million

$875,000 to Investor
$875,000 to Production

Total Investment = $3,000,000

Example of Investor Payout = $4,625,000

Return on Investment over 2 Years (Excluding TV, Pay-Per-View, and Ancillary Markets) = 54.16%

One of the two most important pages in the business plan (along with the risk management page). I'll explain more later, but the key is to be realistic with the return on investment. Even if you think this number could be higher, don't make it too high.

APPENDIX B

BIOS/RESUMES

Put your best foot forward here. Notice this primarily described me as a producer/writer. For this fictional film, my actor bio is not included, because that's not how I'm going to make the HNI money.

TOM MALLOY, WRITER/ACTOR/PRODUCER

Tom Malloy most recently wrote and produced *Love N' Dancing*, directed by Rob Iscove (*She's All That*). The film stars Amy Smart, Billy Zane, Rachel Dratch, and Betty White. The film will be in theatres in May of 2009.

Tom Malloy also recently wrote and produced *The Alphabet Killer*, a psychological thriller directed by Rob Schmidt (*Wrong Turn, Crime & Punishment in Suburbia*). The film stars Eliza Dushku, Cary Elwes, Timothy Hutton, Michael Ironside, and Bill Moseley. The film will be in theatres (limited release) at the end of 2008.

Tom also wrote and produced *The Attic*, a thriller directed by Mary Lambert (director of *Pet Sematary I & II*), and starring John Savage, Jason Lewis, and Elisabeth Moss. Tom also produced *In a Single Bound*, the much-hyped Superman documentary which premiered at the Tribeca Film Festival in 2006.

Inclusive of Tom's other work:

- ◇ The critically acclaimed documentary *High Roller: The Bob Perry Story.*

- ◇ The educational video *The Agony of Ecstasy*, the first and best video on the club drug ecstasy that has sold to over 1000 schools!

- ◇ *The World Championships of Country Dance* (with Robert Royston) for GAC television. The first time country dancing was ever on TV, and it was broadcast to over 34 million homes!

Tom was also one of the lead actors in the film *Gravesend*, produced by Oliver Stone. The film became an indie-cult favorite. He has also appeared in principal roles on *Law & Order, Third Watch, Kidnapped, The Siege* (with Denzel Washington) and *Anger Management.* (*www.TomMalloy.com*)

123 PICTURES, FOREIGN SALES

Founded in March 2002, 123 Pictures is a sales and financing operation formed as a partnership between sales veteran John Smith and producer Jim Jones.

Jones was responsible for such hits as **ABC**, **EFG**, and **HIJ**. He has worked in and around the film business for over 20 years.

Prior to forming 123, Smith was VP of sales and acquisitions at 123 Pictures. He was involved in the sales of many of 123's films, including **The Made Up Title**, **The Fictional Film** with Robert DeNiro, and **The Example Film** with Jennifer Aniston.

In less than five years, 123 Pictures has formed a very successful sales operation with over 100 titles in its library.

Okay, obviously, this is all made up. The bio of your foreign sales company will go here.

Also, you may want to include any other bios that make you sound better and more appealing to investors.

If you have a director attached, make sure to include his or her bio. If it's a first-time director, you have to be smart. If the bio doesn't really say much, leave it out for now. If you have any cast attachments, insert them here as well (if they mean something to the investor).

Just don't include too many bios. I've read business plans containing up to twenty bios. Who is going to read all those? Not the investor.

APPENDIX C

OVERVIEW OF THE FILM INDUSTRY

The film industry consists of two principal activities: production and distribution. Production encompasses the development, financing and creation of feature-length films. Distribution involves the promotion and exploitation of films throughout the world in a variety of media, including theatrical exhibition, home video, television, cable, pay-per-view, satellite, DVD, Internet and other ancillary markets.

The film industry has diversified its revenue sources and grown substantially as a whole in the past two decades, primarily due to technological developments and the growth of international markets. Technological developments have resulted in the availability of alternative distribution media for film entertainment, including expanded pay and cable television, pay-per-view, DVD and the Internet.

Despite the limited resources generally available to independent studios, independent films have gained wider market approval and increased share of overall box office receipts in recent years. Recent successful independent films highlight moviegoers' willingness to support high quality motion pictures despite limited marketing and the absence of "star power."

It is difficult to be specific about the likelihood of the success of a particular film or library of films. Indeed, there are no dependable rules of thumb that provide a guide to making revenue projections for films. However, there has been ten consecutive years of box office growth throughout the world. The economic downturn is squeezing consumer spending, but there's one corner of the consumer pocketbook that'll emerge unscathed from the "r" word. Based on articles that have appeared over time in the film business, moviegoing is pretty much recession-proof: Box office receipts have grown over six of the last seven recessions.

FILM DEVELOPMENT AND PRODUCTION

The production of a film occurs in four distinct phases prior to initial release: development, preproduction, principal photography and postproduction. During the development phase, the producer generally acquires the rights to a novel, story or screenplay or develops the story internally, and finances the writing or the revision of the screenplay.

After a screenplay has been approved for production, the project enters the preproduction phase. During preproduction the producer will engage creative and production personnel, obtain insurance, plan shooting schedules, establish locations, secure any necessary studio facilities, finalize the budget, and prepare for the start of actual filming.

After financing is put in place, the next phase is principal photography. This usually takes 21 to 40 days to complete, depending on such factors as location, weather, budget, special effects, or other unique requirements of the screenplay. Following this, postproduction commences. The film is edited: music, dialogue and special visual effects or audio effects are added, and the voice, other effects and music are synchronized with the photography. The producer utilizes the resulting film negative to create the prints to be released to cinemas.

The producer (either directly or, in most cases in the independent film production sector, via its duly appointed agent) enters into agreements with distributors to distribute the film in designated film markets. The producer and distributors will then develop marketing campaigns and advertising budgets in preparation for the theatrical release of the film.

FILM DISTRIBUTION AND EXHIBITION

Distributing and exploiting films in various markets throughout the world, pursuant to customary release patterns or "windows," generates revenue for films. These windows include domestic and international theatrical exhibition, non-theatrical venues (which include airlines, military installations, hospitals and hotels), home video, U. S.

television (including pay-per-view and pay, network, syndication and basic cable) and other ancillary sources such as consumer products, themed entertainment and publishing, DVD, Internet, other "new media" and music soundtrack sales.

While the timing of revenue received varies for each film, a substantial part of the revenue generated by a film is usually received within the first three years of a film's life, with the majority of such revenue being received within the first 18 months of a film's initial distribution cycle.

PRODUCER'S NET PROFITS

Gross receipts include all proceeds from distribution and exploitation of the film in any existing and future medium. From these gross receipts the sales and marketing agent's fees and expenses are deducted. Next, the providers of finance and investors in the film are entitled to recoup the amount of their investment plus preferential return and other agreed financing costs. Further payments may be made to a completion guarantor if there has been a cost overrun. Finally, payments are made to entities involved in the production process that have agreed to accept deferred payments. Payments accruing to the Producer, following the deduction of the above sums and any other deductions, are termed "Producer's Net Profits." This is the level at which the investors may participate in the profits of a film, although the amount and definition of "Producer's Net Profits" will vary on a film-by-film basis.

SOURCE OF REVENUE

Gross box office receipts are shared between the territorial distributor and theatre owners. The distributor's share of box office receipts is referred to as "theatrical rentals." Box office splits are determined on a film-by-film basis with each exhibitor and are often negotiated based on the box office performance of the producer's prior releases. Although these shares vary widely, on average the split between exhibitor and distributor is 50/50 over the length of the theatrical run.

The principal expenses related to theatrical release are print and advertising (P&A) costs. Print costs are incurred for duplicating the negative into prints that will be sent to theatres for actual exhibition. The processing and distribution of prints depends on the number of screens on which it is initially exhibited. A certain amount of advertising costs are incurred during the two months preceding the theatrical release of a new film, with the majority of advertising costs being incurred just prior to or on release of the film. Advertising costs include the production and placement of print advertisement in magazines and trade publications, television, radio, billboards and the production costs of fifteen-second to two-minute trailers, as well as various publicity and promotional campaigns. Advertising costs to "open" a film (i.e., expenditures incurred to drive awareness of a new film release) are significant and, for a widely released film, may be more than half of the total P&A budget. Although theatrical rentals alone may not justify such expenditures, creating brand identity and awareness for a particular film fosters sales in subsequent release windows, particularly DVD and television.

In addition to the revenue from theatrical release, films may generate revenue that ultimately, the Producer and Investors may share in by way of:

ANCILLARY RIGHTS

Music from the film may be licensed for soundtrack release, public performance or even sheet music publication. Rights may also be licensed to merchandisers for the manufacture of products such as video games, toys, T-shirts, posters and other merchandise. Rights may also be licensed for novelizing the screenplay and other related book publications or instructional videos.

NON-THEATRICAL RIGHTS

Late in the domestic theatrical run, a distributor may license the film for non-theatrical exhibition to distributors who make the film available to airlines, ships, military installations and other governmental institutions.

HOME VIDEO/DVD

A film may be distributed to the home video market utilizing a rental or sell-through strategy. Most of the films are distributed using a rental strategy whereby video cassettes and DVDs are primarily sold to video retailers for rental to members of the public, with the manufacturing of cassettes/DVDs and trade marketing as the principal costs incurred by the distributor.

A sell-through strategy is chosen based on genre and a film's theatrical performance when a producer believes that the number of cassettes/DVDs sold directly to consumers (either in addition to or in place of those sold to video retailers for rental) will create an opportunity to generate profits that will exceed those generated under a rental strategy.

PAY-PER-VIEW, PAY AND FREE TELEVISION

Television rights to films are generally licensed first to pay-per-view in the USA (the UK, Australian, German and other countries' pay-per-view market is only now starting with the recent launch of digital television) following or concurrent with home video release, then to pay television followed by network broadcast television and finally to local broadcast stations or basic cable networks. Producers license their films to pay television networks for a fee based primarily on the film's theatrical performance or to pay-per-view networks for a fee based on the number of consumers who elect to view the film. Free television means the license of the film to terrestrial television (e.g. CBS, NBC, ABC, PBS, BBC, etc.), which is available to the public without payment of a fee or subscription.

REVENUE AND COST TRENDS

The film industry has diversified its revenue sources and grown substantially as a whole in the past two decades, primarily due to technological developments and the growth of international markets. Technological developments have resulted in the availability of alternative distribution media for film entertainment, including expanded pay and cable television, pay-per-view, DVD and the Internet.

It is difficult to be specific about the likelihood of the success of a particular film or library of films. Indeed, there are no dependable rules of thumb that provide a guide to making revenue projections for films. However, there has been ten consecutive years of box office growth throughout the world.

Internationally, box office generally represents less than 25% of the total revenue from film distribution. The "rule of thumb" for distribution revenues is that box office accounts for approximately 22.5% of total receipts, DVD for 55%, and broadcast, pay, cable, syndication, satellite and all other rights for the remaining 22.5%.

THE FUTURE
BOX OFFICE

The domestic box office continued to grow in 2007, reaching $9.63 billion after a 5.4% gain. Worldwide box office reached another all-time high in 2007 with $26.7 billion, a 4.9% increase.

TELEVISION

Television markets have enormous potential for continued growth, especially in developing nation's markets. Free to air channels have been joined by cable and satellite subscription channels that have significant scope for market penetration. Digital television technology means that the home theatre dream is an imminent reality. This market will become increasingly important as digital receivers become less expensive over the next several years. These sets will double as computer screens and provide a complete entertainment, information and educational experience.

HOME VIDEO / DVD

The home viewing preference is forecast to grow even more by the year 2009 as spending on DVDs, fueled by explosive growth in movie purchases as opposed to rentals, increases at 9.1% compound annual rate over the next 5 years. The penetration of DVD players into homes throughout the world continues at a spectacular rate.

DIGITAL – DVD AND THE INTERNET

The DVD and Internet markets are becoming increasingly important as digital television receivers and players will become less expensive over the next several years.

These new digital technologies are set to alter the release pattern windows for film. Until recently, a film would appear in the home video market within 6 months of its theatrical release; 6 months later it might have appeared on the premium pay television networks and a further 12 months later it might have hit the free-to-air television screens.

Recently, the release pattern window exclusively devoted to home video has been expanding. This trend is expected to continue with the growing popularity of DVD. 20th Century-Fox released *Titanic* on DVD shortly after its theatrical run. The other major studios are now doing the same; an example of this might be Disney's huge success with *Pirates of the Caribbean*.

DISTRIBUTION HIGHLIGHTS

Film industry analysts are predicting a period of solid growth in the film market. This growth will be driven by different factors in different areas of the market.

Theatrical revenues are expected to continue their upward trend on the back of:
‹› Population growth
‹› Increasing levels of attendance
‹› Graduated price increase
‹› Multiplexing catering to an "entertainment experience"

DVD/Cable revenues are expected to continue to add growth due to:
‹› The introduction, and expected Advertising penetration, of digital technologies such as Internet delivery and high definition TV receivers

APPENDIX D

NEW FEDERAL TAX LEGISLATION
Immediate Write-off of Expenditures

FREQUENTLY ASKED QUESTIONS

(1) **Q: When do productions need to commence to qualify for the new incentive?**
A: The incentive is available for qualified productions commencing after October 22, 2004, and before January 1, 2009. This incentive has recently been extended for one year.

(2) **Q: Can the immediate write-offs be taken in more than one year?**
A: Yes, if an election is made to use the incentive, the immediate deduction takes place in the year the expenditure is incurred. Therefore, if production expenditures are incurred in more than one year, the immediate tax deduction will be taken in more than one year.

(3) **Q: When, where, and how does the "election" to immediately deduct the qualifying expenditures apply?**
A: The election is to be made on the tax return for the taxable year in which the production costs are first incurred. The election must be made by the due date (including extensions of time) of such return. The manner and form of the election will be determined by the IRS at a later date.

(4) **Q: What is the real benefit of this incentive?**
A: This is a significant new federal tax incentive that allows producers to take a tax deduction for the full costs of a production in the year the cost is incurred (as opposed to having to spread or amortize those costs over a period of years). Deducting the costs up front, while deferring the income from the films until later years when it is incurred, will significantly reduce or eliminate the investor's taxable income for the film in the early years of exploitation.

(5) **Q: Is the incentive transferable?**
A: No. However, different entity structures such as limited liability corporations, partnerships, and others, should be considered to properly allocate costs that could be immediately expensed.

This FAQ was initially drawn up by my producing partners on *Love N' Dancing*. When I placed it into my business plan after refining it and cutting it down, I ran it by an attorney. He told me it was perfect. So I kept it in.

APPENDIX E

SALES PROJECTIONS/REPORTS FOR PREVIOUS FILMS PRODUCED BY TOM MALLOY

Graphs are cool and they add color.

The Attic
Foreign Sales: $125,000 advance, $70,000 sales
Domestic Sales: $75,000 advance
Foreign Projections: $180,000 total by the end of 2008
Domestic Projections: $555,894 total by the end of 2008

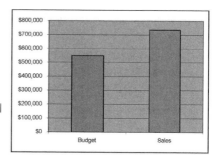

Budget: $550,000
Total Projected Sales: $735,894
ROI... all they need to know.
ROI for Investors: 33.79%

The Alphabet Killer
Foreign Sales: $660,000 already sold
Domestic Sales: $400,000 advanced
Foreign Projections: $2,800,000 total by the end of 2008
Domestic Projections: $1,250,000 total by the end of 2009

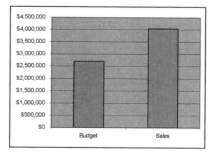

Budget: $2,700,000
Total Projected Sales: $4,050,000
ROI for Investors: 50%

Love N' Dancing
Foreign Sales: $815,000 already sold
Foreign Projections: $2,800,000 total by the end of 2008
Domestic Projections: $9,800,000 total by the end of 2009

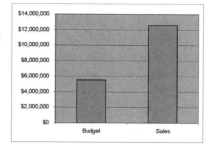

Budget: $5,500,000
Total Projected Sales: $12,600,000
Notice that each ROI got bigger with each film. That's a great sign for an investor.
ROI for Investors: 129%

APPENDIX F

RISK MANAGEMENT DETAILS

Michigan's Current Film Incentives – 40% Tax Credit

‹› 40% cash rebate, across the board on Michigan expenditures, with a spending threshold of $50,000.

‹› Michigan adds an extra 2% if the company films in one of the 103 Core Communities in Michigan.

‹› Labor and Crew: 40%-42% Resident and Above the Line, 30% Non-resident Below the Line.

‹› The only cap will be a maximum of $2 million salary per employee.

‹› There is no other cap and does not terminate.

For any state, you can copy their tax incentive details off of their film commission website. Don't just cut and paste it, though. Make sure all that you're including is relevant info for your film.

For example, is the salary cap line needed?

APPENDIX G

CONTACT INFORMATION

This should go without saying, but make sure all this information is up to date. Nothing will scream "fraud" more to an investor than having a phone number that doesn't exist.

A chance to showcase your amazing website.

Trick Candle Productions
123 Main St., Los Angeles, CA 90000

Tom Malloy
123.456.7890 (p)
tmalloy@bankrollthebook.com

Company fax: 123.456.7890
Company website: *www.trickcandle.com*

Dissecting the Business Plan

Let's go back over each part in more detail:

Executive Summary

This section must be clear and concise. Bulleted so that it reads clean. Only hit your major points.

This is the first area where things may change. If risk management is the highest priority for your HNI, put that near the top. If foreign sales are of no concern to your HNI, cut it. If he or she wants to know about your attachments, place that information up front.

Risk Management Overview

The way the economy is today, and with the state of the independent film market, this page may be the most important one in your document, and it may be how you raise the money.

While Chapter 13: The Structured Approach discusses risk management in detail, it's important for you to note that we're using a tax credit and some foreign sales to minimize the risk for the HNI to only twenty cents on the dollar. That's pretty good.

What's also amazing here is that, due to the tax write-off, you're basically telling your investor that he or she is 100% covered by their investment. Do you realize how powerful this page can be?

Also make sure to note that you're talking about minimum projections (and we're assuming 123 Pictures is a reputable sales company, which will be covered in later chapters). That way, you're telling your investor that he or she will be covered in a worst-case scenario situation.

Previous Films

You may not be able to include this section into the business plan, and that's okay. Selling without previous experience is an obstacle, but not an insurmountable one.

If you do have previous films, list them here as concisely as possible. Report their current or past status, and, if possible, mention what the future holds for them (as I alluded to in the notes).

Project Synopsis

Self-explanatory. Remember that *The Investigator* is not a real film, so I don't want to get any flack for a synopsis I drew up in two minutes!

Box Office & Marketing/Distribution

You're going to give a general overview of what you plan to do with the film once it's been completed. Where are you taking it? How is it going to be sold? If you don't have relationships with distributors, you may want to list the film festivals you'll be submitting to. But you have to have a game plan.

I always put together a chart of previous films that were similar to my own. This definitely places your movie in a positive light. You can find the box office numbers for most films on either IMDbPro or Boxofficemojo. I include the returns these films made. When you're choosing films for your chart, pick the good ones that have good ROIs (return on investments). Here's a formula for calculating the ROI:

ROI = [(Payback - Investment)/Investment)] x 100

For example, if a film whose budget was $4 million grosses $19 million, the ROI would be calculated as follows:

ROI=($19 million-$4 million)/$4 million x 100 = 375%

A 375% ROI is a figure that would thrill any investor.

I remember putting together these charts for *The Attic* and *The Alphabet Killer*. I chose films like *Halloween* and *Texas Chainsaw Massacre* because they were horror films that made ridiculous amounts of money. I left out the bombs. When I was putting together charts for *Love N' Dancing*, I found an interesting piece of information: There wasn't a dance film I could find that didn't make money! So what did I do? I added this little story to the pitch for investors.

Make sure the HNIs do not think that the returns listed in your chart are what they will be getting! The other films I included in my sample business plan did not return those numbers only to their investors. I actually lost a sale this way, because I had not included Appendix A: Example of Investor Payout. The HNI I had approached passed, and I didn't know why. I found out later that he thought the charts were a misrepresentation of the film. He thought I was telling him he'd make a 500% return, and that was too good to be true for him.

SIDE NOTE

Production Plan and Timeline

This Production Plan is pretty self-explanatory. Your reader is likely to skip it, but it still needs to be in there. The Timeline is less likely to be ignored. The investor wants to know when his or her money will be returned. Note that I am just listing the eight-month return (after the completion of the film) as a "goal." Nothing is set in stone here. It's definitely doable, though, if the timing is right.

Appendix A: Projected Investor Return

This page is *so* important. I've had investors just turn to this page and ignore all others. I'd rank this section equal in significance to the risk management page.

One of the keys here is to make your projections fairly conservative. Even if you believe the film is going to make $20 million for the investor, don't show that. He or she will get scared away by a high percentage. In this sample case, you're showing 54%, which is very high, but not ridiculous. Show a 375% ROI, and they'll be likely to run. Many times I've lowered a projection I actually believed in because I thought the HNI would think it was too high. Remember, in the investing world, a 20% return is a high return!

Make sure that your calculation for the investor payout is clearly marked as an "example." You don't want your figures to be brought back up to you if you haven't returned your HNI's money. Or worse, you don't want your HNI suing you. A true HNI most likely retains a highly paid attorney or team of attorneys and suing you would be a piece of cake.

Appendix B: Bios/Resumes
This section is self-explanatory and detailed in the plan.

Appendix C: Overview of the Film Industry
This section is self-explanatory and detailed in the plan.

Appendix D: Tax Legislation Incentive
Remember, this is active at the time of the writing, and it's up for renewal. But this can be a very important page to an HNI who needs a big write-off.

Budgets

The business plan above included a budget of $3 million. In the independent film world, most budgets are derived by "backing in." This means a specific number, let's say $3 million, is chosen, and the budget for your film is created by "backing in" to that number, meaning you make your film doable for $3 million.

This is not the proper method of carrying out business, obviously, but it is by far the most common way in the independent film world. When I write or read a script, I get a general idea in my head of what the film can be shot for. However, that's not always the amount that I try to raise.

Sometimes you'll derive your budget numbers via your knowledge of your HNI. For example, let's say I had targeted someone and felt that $500,000 was the most he could do. At that point, I would fashion a script around that $500,000, or, if I already had a script, change it (if necessary) to reflect a $500,000 budget.

You can also use a more scientific approach to create specific budgets. Contact a line producer. Good ones can be found through IMDbPro or *www.Mandy.com*. As always, make sure you qualify this person by checking his or her credits and potentially reaching out to your "ring." (More on the "Ring" in Chapter 8: Starting the Train.)

If you're having trouble qualifying the person, or you don't want to commit, you don't have to. Instead of hiring him or her for the whole project, just have the person put together some budgets for you. I made "budget" plural because you need more than one. In some cases, I have three budgets constructed:

◊ Dream budget: If I could get this amount, everything would be perfect. I'd be able to hire whomever I wanted, involve all the unions, and afford a lot of A-list talent.

◊ Good budget: This amount would be enough to make the movie without cutting all the corners. It's the best way to be safe, involve some unions, and afford some good names as far as talent is concerned.

◊ Get 'Er Done Budget: This is the bottom-line dollar amount necessary to make the film. Every corner would have to be cut. A lot of the crew would have to be non-union. You'd still be able to attract talent, but conditions would be rough. Expect some gray hairs after it's done, but, at the end of the day, you'll have a film.

I can say realistically that 90% of all indie filming is done with this last budget.

Don't think just because your budget is low you won't be able to attract talent! I have always had luck getting stars to work for indie wages, and you should have the same luck if/when your film gets financed. How is this possible? If you have a killer script! Also, if you have an experienced director, it's a lot easier for the talent to say, "Well, he or she won't make me look bad." It also helps if your casting director is reputable.

Keep in mind that most proposed film projects are pipe dreams, lacking both the financing and the talent attached to secure funds. So, when you do get your film going, you're bound to get stars because there are not that many projects out there. Actors want to work (trust me), and the jobs are getting fewer and further between. As evidence, note that even major film celebrities are now making television guest appearances (Robin Williams was on *Law & Order* in 2008; this never would have happened ten years ago). Bottom line: Get your film financed to any degree, and you will be able to get some major talent.

The Get 'Er Done budget is more accurately called the Minimum Cost Budget (MCB). This is a very important number to know. Let's say you're presenting a business plan for $3 million. If you had $4 million, it would be a dream budget, but $3 million will suffice for your good budget.

Now, take your MCB, which is $2 million — the lowest you'd be willing to go — and make sure you know that you can make that film for that money. That number becomes important in your pitch. I've worked these figures into Operating Agreements and Offering Memorandums (more detail on this later in the chapter). Basically, I'm telling the investor that if and when we hit $2 million, no matter what, the film will get made. It's the minimum we have to raise to make the film. At that point, we will continue to try to raise enough money so that we have $3 million, but the investor can take comfort in the fact that the film will be produced.

Sometimes the minimum cost budget becomes a necessity. Let's say you landed an investor for $1 million, and your film was budgeted at $3 million. No matter how hard you try, you can't get the other $2 million. An option is to rewrite the script, cut a bunch of corners, and just go for it. "Back in" to the $1 million and make a movie. You can also use the $1 million to get the film in the can, and leave out the post-production budget. While in post, you can look for finishing funds.

The only time you *cannot* stop the ball rolling is when you are in production. Development can last for an eternity. Preproduction can last for as long as you want it to last, as long as you don't have a deadline on money or pay-or-play actors. Postproduction can also last as long as you want, as long as you don't have a deadline on returning money or a paying off a bridge loan. But, if you try to stop production, you're dead in the water. Production is like a gigantic rock rolling down a hill. It's almost impossible to stand in its way, and if you do, you'll most likely get crushed.

SIDE NOTE

Would you rather just have that money sitting in a bank, or worse, have to give it back? Always choose to make a movie!

Give yourself a deadline to raise your dream budget or your good budget, but always go back to the MCB so that, at the end of the day, you've got a film.

Operating Agreements and Offering Memorandums

The business plan that I have included is a Confidential Information Overview (CIO). Its purpose is to provide information on an investment, but it cannot be used as paperwork to get the investment.

If I showed this business plan to an investor and he or she said, "I'm in," I would have to produce two important documents: the Operating Agreement for the LLC (Limited Liability Company), and the Offering Memorandum (sometimes referred to as the Private Placement Memorandum). Every film you make will have a separate LLC. It would be insane to make multiple films under the same LLC and try to worry about which accounting statements go to which film. The Operating Agreement will dictate the rules of the LLC and how your company will be operating. The Offering Memorandum will explain the specific offer of the investment. That's the document your investor will sign.

A lawyer must draft or approve both of these documents. In the past, I've recycled old Operating Agreements and Offering Memos by simply changing around the wording. Then I've run the new document by an attorney, and thus saved money on the countless hours he or she was going to charge by drafting it from scratch (but I'd almost bet attorneys do the same thing and recycle old boilerplate documents). I highly suggest the second method, because then all the lawyer has to do is make slight changes and approve the documents.

These documents are essential, but I'm not going to advise you to go out right now and start paying to get them drafted. I've almost always sold the investor on a CIO (Confidential

Information Overview), and then, when he or she is ready to close, I go get the official papers. This is where turnaround time has to be quick, however. If your lawyer is slow, get rid of him or her. There's no room for "slow" in the film business.

Let's say I was pitching an investor on the business plan we just saw and, right away, the HNI were to respond, "Okay, let's do it. I want to invest $3 million." I would say "Great! I'll have the documents to you within forty-eight hours." Then I would rush home, abandon everything else I had to do that day, and start to make changes to the old Operating Agreements and Offering Memos I have, if I hadn't done it already.

> If you use the recycling method, it's much easier to have the documents ready to go. Get them as finished as you can make them so, as soon as you have an investor on the hook, all you have to do is run them by a lawyer who will finalize them.

SIDE NOTE

After that, I will send the documents off to my lawyer and wait for him to get back to me. I actually employ three different attorneys at the present time, and each has his own strength and weakness. One is a speed demon. Another is a contractual wizard if you need something from scratch. The third charges the least! In the case of the $3 million budget movie I just described, I would send it to the speed demon, and tell him, I need this ASAP!

If he gave me any gruff (which many lawyers do), I'd ask him, "Should I just throw this to one of my other guys?" It's not a threat. I make it clear that the document needs to get done no matter what, and I have to consider that the top priority. This approach almost always does the trick because the lawyer doesn't want to lose the work. I have a reputable lawyer friend who tells his clients when he's too busy and actually advises them to have a backup legal counsel. I can understand if the lawyer is working on something more important or is too busy, but ultimately it's not my concern. All I care about is getting the document I need and finding the person who can do this for me. There's no room for favorites and niceties here.

SIDE NOTE

I'm notoriously tough on lawyers. I can't pinpoint why, but I think it stems from the fact that they charge you for everything, including when they blow their noses. Friends and family call me up for computer advice almost weekly, and I give it to them without even a thought. I've rarely had lawyers do that for me, and when they do, they always point out how they could be charging me. Is this something they teach in law school? That legal work is more important and intricate than any other profession? Yeah, right.

When I need a contract, I stay on top of my lawyers constantly, so I can make sure they're not running up a huge hourly tab. I find it funny that producers who are former lawyers are even harder on attorneys than I am. Maybe they understand how easy it is to slack off. I think one day I will get a law degree just so I can do all my own contracts and yell at myself. But remember, it's okay to be tough on them. *You* are the client. They are there to serve you, and some need to be reminded of this.

The bottom line here is that these documents, the Operating Agreement and the Offering Memorandum, are very necessary, but I consider them almost a formality. The art of film financing is not rooted in your facility with legal documents. It's all about salesmanship, and if you read any book on this topic, you'll understand that selling is all about selling yourself. By the time I'm "going to paper" (presenting contracts) with an investor, he or she is already sold.

In Closing — Some Rules for Your Business Plan

1) You need to know your business plan in and out. If an HNI is asking you questions about the plan, are you going to have to say, "Hold on, let me check"? Does that project confidence? Don't be caught off guard.

2) If anything new comes up, add it into the plan. It's a great way to reconnect with people to whom you've already sent the plan. Email this:

> Hey, NAME,
> We just attached director Steven Spielberg to the project. I've updated the business plan to reflect this. Let me know what you think!

That would be a nice email to send.

3) Always keep the date updated, even if nothing has changed. If I get a business plan in May and it says January on it, all that's telling me is that you've been trying to fund it for five months with no success. There has to be a freshness about the business plan.

4) Notice that I haven't included a budget top sheet. This is purposely left out. Save that for the Offering Memorandum. At this point, seeing too detailed a budget can be confusing and overwhelming to an investor. Always have it ready, though, in case he or she requests it.

5) Don't make the business plan too long! I've seen fifty- and sixty-page business plans. Do you really think an investor is going to read all this? I assume the aim here is to impress the investor with your massive document. I haven't seen this work. Most of the time, these massive documents are weighed down unnecessarily, through poor choices like giving each section of the plan its own cover page.

6) Make sure the layout and the design is visually appealing. If you don't trust yourself on this (and you probably shouldn't), run it by a graphic designer. A great idea is to pay to have a logo designed, and to hire a professional to lay out the page in a presentable way.

7) Make sure it's printed on nice paper and bound. Also make sure it's in color. Would you rather get a business plan that's stapled and copied in black and white?

8) Always, always, submit your business plan for legal review. I've included a CIO Disclaimer that was created for me by an entertainment attorney. Don't just cut and paste this! You need to have your attorney go over every aspect of the plan and make sure you're not exposed to any potential liability. Be tough on your lawyer! That's what you're paying him or her for.

◇ ◇ ◇

Okay, so you've got your killer script, you're sold on the project, and you've got your business plan to back it up. Now you need to create your pitch.

PRACTICING
YOUR PITCH

6

Are You Ready?

Let's say it's 2 a.m. and you're at a bar or a dance club. You've had some drinks and it's the end of the night, so you're tired. As you slowly make your way to pay your tab, you find yourself standing next to a guy who's dressed to the nines. You strike up a conversation and he tells you he's a commercial real estate developer and he's worth $40 million. Then he asks you what you do and you tell him you're a filmmaker. He asks, "What are you working on?"

Are you ready? Can you seamlessly flow into your pitch? Are you able to shake off the effects of the alcohol and tiredness and start selling this guy on why he should give you $1 million of his hard-earned $40 million fortune?

You have to be. There can be no "should'ves" when you're raising money for your film. I have bragged in the past that I could be awakened at 3 a.m. with a flashlight aimed at me by a home intruder who demands, "Pitch me your feature film!" I would take a deep breath, and then start the pitch. It has to be second nature. It must be natural and easy and it's got to flow.

The pitch is your friend. It gets you paid and gets your film made. It's the gift that you are giving to an investor.

You never know where or when you're going to meet the person who will invest in your movie. You may be standing in line at the airport. You may be sitting in a dentist's office. You may be waiting for your car to get fixed. You have to be armed with your pitch at all times.

I had one investor who was a heavy drinker. He liked to call me up at 11 p.m. and ask me to come over to his house. One time I was in bed with my wife, ready to go to sleep. He sent me a text asking me to come over and talk about the film. I got up, got dressed, and got ready. When I got to his house, we started doing shots.

After about the third shot, he asked me to start talking about the film, and that's exactly what I did. You see, I take this business very seriously. I've seen many weak producers just get trashed and lose sight of the prize. I never do. When I'm pitching a film, I could have thirty shots! (Okay, that may be a slight exaggeration.) I know that making films is what feeds my family and pays for my house. So I took a deep breath, and started the pitch. I got a verbal commitment for several million dollars that night.

The Most Important Element

Your excitement is the most crucial element of your pitch. Think about it. You're asking this person to give you his or her hard-earned money. Do you think you'll get what you want if you're just flat when you talk about your film? How about if you say something like the following:

> "Yeah, well I've got this film going and it could be pretty good. We think we'll get a nice cast and maybe make a little bit of money."

I don't know about you, but I don't think I would invest in that project. I don't want to be associated with a film that's "pretty good" and will make a "little bit" of money. So let's change it. How about this:

> "We have this amazing film going… it's so exciting! This film could turn out to be the next *Saw*! We're gonna get a topnotch cast and crew and whoever invests is gonna make a huge return!"

Okay, now I'm listening! This film is "amazing, exciting" and could turn out to be the next *Saw*! And, if I invest, I can make a huge Return on Investment? Wow!

Now here's the thing: Those two pitches you just read might be for the same exact movie! It's just that the first was given by someone who wasn't excited and the second by someone who was. Remember what we discussed in Chapter 3: What No One Else Can Do? If you truly believe that you are letting this person in on a gift, you would be excited. You should be excited…. Hell, you need to be excited!

What if I gave you $10,000 and told you to go to a restaurant, pick out a female diner you feel most deserves the money, and give it to her? If you carried out my request, I'd also give you $10,000. Do you think you'd be excited? As you were telling the diner that she would be receiving $10,000 for doing nothing, do you think she would be excited? Of course!

Excitement translates. People pick up on your passion and positive energy and they start feeling it too. Investors want you to be passionate about your project when you pitch it to them, because they want to make a good investment. If you're relaxed and trying to "play it cool," it just may not work. Go play it cool with your friends at a bar while the people who geek out on their pitches get their films made.

I will admit that I completely geek out when I'm pitching. I've been known to jump up on chairs (a la Tom Cruise). The person I'm pitching immediately picks up on my enthusiasm and starts to feel it as well.

Do *not* confuse this with the used-car salesman approach, where the salesperson fakes his passion, because, deep down, he doesn't believe the project will sell. An investor will pick up on this in a heartbeat! Go back to Chapter 4: Selling Yourself on the Project. When I'm pitching and telling an investor that I'm going to double his money, I truly believe — with complete conviction — that's what I'm going to do, and that that translates to the investor. You have to believe in yourself and get excited and passionate in order to sell! There's no better lesson I can impart to you.

Some of My Pitches

It's tough to define exactly what needs to be in your pitch, because there are so many variables. What is your film about? Have similar films made money? Who is starring in it? Who's directing? You'll have covered all of this extensively in the business plan, but you need to have a quick pitch that you can whip out verbally at any time. I'll go over some of pitches I have used to raise money successfully:

Pitch for *The Attic*:

"I have this amazing scary movie called *The Attic*. I've been a horror fan my whole life, and I really feel this is going to be the next *Halloween*! The script is so freakin' scary! I wrote it so that it's totally low-budget and we can get the most bang for your buck. It takes place in one house! We've already got the director of *Pet Sematary* attached to direct, and we're lining up an incredible cast. The budget is only $500,000!"

Pitch Analysis

"Amazing scary movie"
I really did think that *The Attic* was so ready to break out and become a hit.

"I've been a horror fan my whole life"
It's true! And, in the investor's eyes, perhaps I just established myself as an expert.

"The script is so freakin' scary"
People coming in to audition said they couldn't read the script when they were alone!

"Wrote it so that it's totally low-budget"

Again, just like the previous statements, this is 100% true. I had the budget in mind as I was writing the script and set the film in one location (a house), and only wrote a total of about ten characters.

"We've already got the director of *Pet Sematary*"

We had Mary Lambert attached based on the strength of the script, and she was a huge win for our little independent film.

"We're lining up an incredible cast"

I had seen the submissions for the film, and they were looking great.

"The budget is only $500,000"

I truly believed, with a budget this small and with the people behind this film, we would make millions for our investors.

As stated in Chapter 1, I think there were mistakes made in the actual filming of *The Attic*. It turned out to be an art house film more than a horror movie, but hindsight is 20/20 and, at this point, I'm only talking about the pitch. When I was pitching the film, I truly believed it was going to be the next *Halloween*. That fact translated to the people I was pitching the film to, and they decided to invest. Unfortunately, the movie gods didn't shine on the film, but, at the end of the day, we'll still have made some profit for our investors (which is all that matters), and we produced a film with great performances.

Pitch for *The Alphabet Killer:*

"There's this insane unsolved serial killer case from Rochester, New York. In the 1970s, a guy killed three little girls, aged ten to twelve, who had the same first and last initial. Then he buried them in towns corresponding to that initial. They never found the guy! So I wrote this awesome crime thriller that centers on the lead detective in the case! We can shoot this film for around $2 million. We have Rob Schmidt attached to direct, whose last film, *Wrong Turn*, made $51 million! We also have Eliza Dushku attached to play the lead role, and she has a gigantic fan base! There are so many other great roles in the script, and our casting director is the same person who cast *The Exorcism of Emily Rose*, *The Grudge*, and *Hostel*! We're gonna knock this one out of the park!"

Pitch Analysis

"There's this insane unsolved serial killer case from Rochester, New York"
Okay, this one started a little differently. I wanted to pique interest in the investor by mentioning the real, unsolved case. Turns out the main investor was a huge fan of true crime.

"We can shoot this film for around $2 million"
I'm saying here that it's such a big scope of a film and has so much potential, yet we still can do it for such a low fee! It's a little risky using the word "around," but if the HNI asked for more specifics, I'd be ready with a budget.

"We have Rob Schmidt"
Notice I mentioned the gross of his last film.

"We have Eliza Dushku"
Notice I mentioned her huge fan base.

"Our casting director is the same person who cast"
I wanted to bring up the last three films she cast. All of them were monster hits at the box office, and were listed in the business plan.

"We're gonna knock this one outta the park"
I truly believed it, and I think the end result was that we did.

Photo by Barbara Spoettel

Eliza Dushku and me in a scene from The Alphabet Killer.

The Alphabet Killer turned out to be an incredible film. It's very much like David Fincher's *Zodiac*, but a lot tighter and way less boring. And, we have a payoff, unlike *Zodiac*. I'm not ruining *Zodiac*'s story.... The killer was never found. With ours, though, I came up with a way to make sure you know who the killer is by the end of the film.

Unfortunately, we ran into the same problem many film-makers have been encountering. No studio wants to take a risk on an indie film anymore. I'm 100% confident that if a studio like Sony got behind *The Alphabet Killer* and released it to 2000 screens, it would make an enormous amount of money. But we couldn't get the acquisitions people to take the risk. Pretty much every major studio offered us a video deal, but that's not what this film deserved. It's too bad. Our $2 million film looks like a $15 million film. Thankfully, I was able to get a deal with a fantastic little company named Anchor Bay. Cassian Elwes, who co-heads William Morris Independent, was our sales agent. He helped negotiate the deal.

Anchor Bay was so excited about the film. The advance we received on the film was eight times that of *The Attic*, so we must have done something right. But I will always be proud of this kickass little film.

SIDE NOTE

Two of my horror film idols, Stephen King and Jonathan Demme, both saw *The Alphabet Killer* and were big fans! Stephen even wrote a letter saying how much he liked the film. That was an accomplishment for me.

Pitch for *Love N' Dancing*:

"I have this dance film/romantic comedy that's going to be the next *Dirty Dancing*! It's so huge! This is gonna be the best dancing you've ever seen on film! The style of dance is called West Coast Swing, and it's this smooth, slinky version of swing that's danced to hip-hop, pop, R&B, and country! Pretty much every style of music out there! Look, if we were making a salsa movie, we'd be asking people to like that style of music, like those clubs, and like that scene. With our film, we're showing this awesome dance that can be danced every-where to pretty much any song played on the radio! We think we could start a whole new era in dance and this could be the next disco! We have Rob Iscove attached to direct. His big hit was *She's All That*, which made $150 million and started the whole "teen movie" trend. The guy has been around danc-ing his whole life.... He choreographed the movie *Jesus Christ*

Superstar back in 1974! We're looking to raise $5 million. Dance films are literally bulletproof at the box office! The average gross for the last seven dance films was $130 million!"

Pitch Analysis

"Gonna be the next *Dirty Dancing*"

Right away, I'm comparing it to a film that was one of the most successful independent films of all time, and is Lionsgate's biggest title. With its mere $6 million budget, it has make over $170 million in theatres, not to mention its astronomical video and soundtrack numbers.

"This is the best dancing you're ever gonna see on film"

A bold statement, but I completely believed it, and, after seeing the end result, I still believe it! We got all the world champions of West Coast Swing in our film, and they look incredible. I was such a big fan of West Coast Swing before the movie was made, so I was already set to go crazy for this style of dance once it was seen on film.

"Look, if we were making a salsa movie..."

I said this next section to investors about 7253 times. I could literally recite this in my sleep. It was always my intention to make *Love N' Dancing* a "movement" film. Much like *Karate Kid* inspired countless little kiddies to take karate lessons, and much like *Saturday Night Fever* had everyone in the country doing the hustle, I always felt that *Love N' Dancing* would change dancing in this country. This came across when I was pitching the investment because I knew we were making a film about a dance accessible to all people, no matter what music they liked.

"We have Rob Iscove attached"

Notice I mentioned the gross of his most successful film. I also mentioned the link that he has to dance movies. So important.

"Dance films are bulletproof"

Okay, so I just stated the budget of $5 million. Now I want the investor to know how much I believe in this genre of film. That's a true statement about the past seven dance films. And most of that group had no plot and bad acting! They also had studios behind them, but, at this point, while I was pitching the film, I firmly believed that a studio would be behind us as well.

I couldn't be more proud of *Love N' Dancing*. It's so bright and beautiful, and it's so commercial. It looks like a $20 million film. It's also very funny. Billy Zane provides most of the comic relief, with Rachel Dratch coming in a close second. Amy Smart and I have definite chemistry on the screen. It's all there.

Again, we ran into problems because no one is taking risks on independent films, but we did manage to get someone to go for it. (I will also mention that, again, we got video offers from almost every major studio out there.) Screen Media Films, in conjunction with Universal Home Entertainment, picked up *Love N' Dancing* for a May 2009 release. From early on, I have firmly believed that this film would break out and create a whole new dance trend.

For the purposes of this book, the end results of my films don't matter. All that counts is that I got them financed. These pitches worked. Let me also add that they, like the business plan, were dynamic. Maybe an investor needed to be pitched on the risk management. Maybe an investor wanted to hear about stars. But the core elements were always there. Be ready!

Your Pitch

Okay, so I've revealed the past three investor pitches that I used. Obviously, I would change them up slightly, depending on whom I was pitching. A pitch, just like a script and a business plan, has to be dynamic. As more of the cast became set, I would make sure to include the new names in the pitch. I would push any aspect of the film that I could, and I was constantly thinking about what to add to the pitch to make it sell even more. For instance, one night I was watching a film called *Wolf Creek*, a mediocre horror flick based on a true story. I checked out its gross online and it turns out this film, made for $1 million, grossed $16.2 million in theaters. *The Alphabet Killer* was a true story that I felt was more compelling than *Wolf Creek*. So I compared our film to it and used this information in the pitch.

Practice your pitch as much as you can. Have it running in your head. The more you prepare, the better off you'll be. Be ready to expand upon it, change it, and add to it. If someone points to a hole in your pitch, mend that hole and have the defense ready for next time. If you're pitching that you have director Jake Jones attached to direct, and the investor says, "But his last film bombed," what do you say? Go to director Jones and ask him why he thinks it flopped. When you get that explanation, add that to the pitch.

Let me convey a clear example of this. We had attached Rob Iscove to direct *Love N' Dancing*, and I knew right away he was the perfect director. A former dancer, he had been around dance his whole life. One of the investors I was pitching to brought up the fact that Rob's last film, the *American Idol* movie *From Justin to Kelly*, was a total failure.

The first thing I did was rent the movie, and confirmed, yes, it was practically unwatchable. The second thing I did was to talk to Rob Iscove and ask him what happened. Please note that I am just relaying this story as it was told to me. Turns out the studio wanted a "name" director attached and paid Rob a huge fee. When Rob got to the set, he wasn't allowed to make any script notes, or even consult in any way.

He was just a figurehead. On top of that, Kelly Clarkson could care less about being an actress and was only doing the film because *American Idol* was forcing her to be there. When the film was complete, Fox turned its back on it and refused to run even one ad for the movie during *American Idol*. The film bombed.

A feasible explanation, and I thank God we stuck with Rob because he did an incredible job directing *Love N' Dancing*

Now here's how I spun this potential problem into a positive note for us:

> "You're not gonna believe how we got a big studio direc-tor like Rob Iscove to direct our film. It turns out that Rob's last film was a bomb… the *American Idol* movie, *From Justin to Kelly*. The studio basically hired him as a name director and didn't let him do anything. The bottom line is, because that film wasn't successful, he's looking for a film to be his "comeback" film, and he's chosen to direct ours for like one-fifth the fee of what he normally gets!"

I took what could have been a damaging note in the pitch and turned it around. You have to be able to do this with whatever arises. The best strategy is to identify and attack the problem.

Things to Remember

◊ Truly believe in what you are pitching.
◊ Be excited.
◊ Be willing to change up a pitch if it's not working.
◊ Deal with any obstacles, attack them, and spin them in a positive way.

◊ Have passion!
◊ NSP: **N**ever **S**top **P**itching! (This is my spin on the sales motto "ABC" — **A**lways **B**e **C**losing.)

One of my favorite stories about what it takes to be successful involves a real estate salesman who was having a tough time. Turns out this guy would take it very personally when people said no. It would ruin his day and put him into a depression and he wouldn't get anything done. So one day a master salesman approached him and they discussed the problem. The master salesman asked, "How many 'noes' do you get before you get a 'yes'?"

The depressed real estate salesman thought about this and said, "About thirty. I get 30 'noes' to every one 'yes.'"

So the master salesman taught him a new technique. "If all it takes is thirty 'noes' to get to one 'yes,' you should be elated every time you get a 'no.' Each 'no' is one step closer to you getting a 'yes.' Think about it as if you need to 'collect the noes.'"

The depressed real estate salesman took this advice and made it work for him. Soon, he was the top salesman in the office, because he was using the technique of "collecting the noes."

I've had so many 'noes' in my time in the film business, I cannot count them. (Including probably 300 auditions as an actor where I didn't get the part.) But I always use the aforementioned technique. I collect the "no" in my mind and believe that it is just one step closer to getting a "yes." This is a marvelous strategy and one that I suggest you use on a daily basis while you are pitching. Be happy with the "no."

A "no" is almost better than a "maybe," because most "maybes" are what I call "postponing the no." For whatever reason, the person doesn't have the desire to tell you "no."

Maybe he or she doesn't want to hurt your feelings, or is interested in keeping you on the hook, just in case. Who can tell? A maybe is uncertain. A "no" allows you to move on and get ready for the next time.

Even when you get a no, you've just taken one step closer. You got to practice your pitch and will be stronger, more prepared, and more excited the next time.

FINDING
THE MONEY

7

Money Is All Around Us

You have to believe that we live in an abundant universe and there is more money than we need. You have to be able to tap into that money and use it for your feature film.

The first thing you need to do is create a database of contacts you can approach for money. You'll learn about the networking aspect of how to reach the money people in Chapter 10: The Finder's Fee Approach. But for now, I want you to make a list of everyone who could potentially give you money for your film. Even if you think they are a long shot, put them in the list.

You don't have to use fancy computer programs for this database. I've done a lot of it on index cards. But I have used Microsoft Excel to keep track of whom I called and when I called them.

Setting Up the Excel Database

These are the following column headers in my databases. You can add or subtract whichever ones you need to best serve your efforts.

◇ Name
◇ Company
◇ Title (e.g., Head of Acquisitions)
◇ First Name (key for doing mail merges)
◇ Last Name

◊ Phone
◊ Email
◊ Comments
◊ First Call
◊ Last Call
◊ Next Call

Mail Merges

A mail merge involves sending a form letter or email to everyone in your database. I highly suggest you learn this feature in Microsoft Word or whatever program you use. Word does mail merges with Excel and Outlook, enabling me to send emails to as many people as I have in the database.

Notice that I have an Excel column for just the first name. In the mail merge, you can specify the header:

Dear <<First Name>>,
That will guarantee that you're sending the letter as:

Dear Allison, (or whatever the name is in that column),
What this avoids is the header that screams, "This is a form letter!" I get them all the time:

Dear Tom Malloy,
Or...

Dear Trick Candle Productions,

Some people don't even bother to do a mail merge. They just add me on a list and cc everyone, exposing everyone's email addresses to each person receiving the document. Not a good idea. I've mistakenly cc'd celeb friends on emails and both times I got yelled at. If you send a bulk email this way, you're lazy and foolish, and you might have already alienated part of your audience.

If someone does cc you on a bulk email, you may want to copy all those cc'd into a database, as they are obviously associated with the film business. The sender just exposed his or her database to you.

Go Until No

"Go Until No" is an extremely important sales technique that was taught to me by a master salesman in New Jersey. It instructs you to never stop pitching the sale until the potential client says, "No." I use this technique all the time. If I call on someone and don't hear from him, I wait one week and call on him again. I will continue this process as long as it takes (the week is important to avoid the impression of harassment). You may think it's ridiculous to stay in the game that long, but I know two monster investors who came onboard my films because one of my producing partners or I never let them go.

Even if I get a "no," I still ask if I can contact the potential investor when the project has more attachments, or if it's okay to call for future projects. Never let any prospective HNI go. Once that name is in your database, keep it there forever. I can't imagine taking someone out of there, unless he or she said to me, or sent in an email, "I'm never investing in anything you're associated with, ever!" Jeez, and if I hear that, I guess I'm doing something wrong!

What follows are the tricks that I use. I'm really giving away trade secrets here, and I truly hope you can use them to fund your movie.

Trick #1: Build the Network

A couple years back, I was thinking about where I could find HNIs and I started looking around my office. Right on my desk was *Shield and Diamond*, the official magazine of Pi Kappa Alpha, the fraternity that I was in at college. I started flipping through the pages, and discovered that hundreds of Pi Kappa Alpha national alumni were listed in the back, along with the jobs they currently held. Their personal contact information (and email addresses) was also included. So, what did I do?

I did the busy work that I am famous for and collected all of their names into a database. I created a form letter saying who I was and that I was looking for investors, and I made sure to mention that I was a fraternity brother. I blasted it out to the few hundred emails and got two major leads. One invested $50,000. It was a small sum, but it was something. And $50,000 for maybe four hours of work is well worth it. That was two years ago, and my pitches and projects have gotten much stronger since.

Were you in a fraternity or sorority? Was it national? If so, great; you've got thousands of contacts. This is just one way to get names, numbers, and most important, email addresses.

SIDE NOTE

I always prefer sending an email. Maybe it's the writer in me. I never felt I was the master of the phone, and, truthfully, I would get embarrassed to ask the hard questions such as, "Will you invest?" on the telephone, whereas I'd easily ask it several times via email. Email is also less invasive. But, if the phone is your forte, by all means, use it!

When sending emails, please, please, please use the program's spellcheck feature! Nothing makes you look less professional than writing a sentence such as:

"My film will play in movee theaters accross the country."

No, it won't. If you can't even use spellcheck, my bet is that you don't have the focus and intelligence it takes to produce a film. The way people send emails is very strange. They sometimes just type off the top of their heads and push "Send." I never do. I write the email, then re-read it, then re-write it. And I always use spellcheck. This process is essential to your being regarded as professional and sharp, and to have your emails taken seriously.

Another great way to build the network is to find the email addresses of the top people you want to contact. I've had incredible success with this. If you go to IMDbPro, you can only sometimes find the email address of the high level contact you're after. But if you find out that the pattern for the email address is constructed in a certain way, you can make assumptions as to what your contact's email will be.

For example, let's say you wish to contact Carl Jones, the head of Purple Pictures (all made up). You see that the domain is *purplepictures.com*. The only email address you can find on IMDb is *info@purplepictures.com* (I would rarely send an email to this address, especially where large companies are concerned). The first thing you do is Google: "@purplepictures.com", and see what email addresses come up. Most likely, it will be someone who is not that high up in the company. If you find the email address for Tom Malloy and it's *tmalloy@purplepictures.com*, you can make the assumption that the email address for Carl Jones is *cjones@purplepictures.com*.

Most of the time, email addresses all follow the same pattern rules. Trust me, I was a former information technology guy. There are always exceptions, however. Carl Jones may want his email address to be theboss@purplepictures. com, but you're going to find that, most of the time, you'll be successful.

Often you can also find high-level emails addresses by Googling the person's name and the domain, such as: "Bob Jones @purplepictures.com." That search, consisting of three words, spaced apart, may yield the email address you are looking for.

Trick #2: Associations

One of the smartest things you can do is join an association that deals with an aspect of your movie. Right away, the people in that association will have a vested interest in the success of your project.

For instance, more than 50% of our investors for *Love N' Dancing* are dancers. We made sure to pitch the movie all over the dance world because we knew that everyone in that arena would love to see a film about West Coast Swing succeed.

SIDE NOTE

If you're an actor and you wish to get over the obstacle of starring in your own film, try to "job secure" yourself by making your role something only you can do! For *Love N' Dancing*, I had been dancing West Coast Swing for eight years on and off, and it was a very difficult dance! You've heard my Matt Damon line twice now, I believe.

I suggest this job security technique to people I meet who are wannabe moviestars. My friend Matt is an actor and also a professional magician. I told him to write a script about professional magic. And, if he can't write, find a script about a magician or have it penned for him. Right away, he'd be eliminating that obstacle and giving himself a little more job security. This also works from a director's perspective. If you're directing a movie about skateboarding, and you were a professional skateboarder, investors will have faith that you will be able to pull it off.

Is your film about an issue or a cause? Let's say it involves animal research. Go to a related organization and try to raise money there. Join up with several groups attached to animal research and start to network. Is your project about dirt bikes? Go to BMX! It's such a logical step, yet no one seems to do it! You have to realize that people have a vested interest in what they love.

Trick #3: Dentists

It has become a joke, (due partly to Dov Simens' fantastic and highly recommended book *From Reel to Deal*), but the truth is that dentists do have a lot of disposable income. And, thanks to section 181 of the Jobs Creation Act of 2004 (which is in effect at the time of this writing), investing in film is a tax write-off. Toward the end of the year, HNIs need that tax write-off, and a lot of dentists qualify as HNIs.

The best part of selling your film on the write-off is that the person usually doesn't care if the film succeeds or not. I've actually used the question, "Do you want to give the money to me to make a film, or do you want to give the money to the government?" That's a powerful question!

SIDE NOTE

The Internet White Pages will list all the dentists in a particular area. You can go to their websites and find personal email addresses. Another way to do this is to use something called a Spider program (see the next section for more details).

Trick #4: List Building and Buying

You can get a lot of lists of HNIs on the Internet. The key is, you really have to qualify the company that's supplying the list. If the list is truly opt-in (meaning the person chose to be included in emails about potential investments), it can be very powerful. It's a situation of "you get what you pay for," and this method could cost you. I once rented a list (no reputable company is going to give you their list or you'd just keep blasting it), for $500 and they were going to blast 5000 people with a web page. The page pitched the film that I was trying to raise money for, and had a form to fill out at the bottom for those who wanted more information.

Make sure a lawyer reviews the language on the web page. You can easily risk violating securities laws by extending investments to everyone. The key is that you are just offering "more information." Have a lawyer check it out first to determine if you're safe.

When the blast was complete, I had three leads and followed up on each. None invested, but I was able to get one to speak on the phone, and I really thought he was going to come through. He didn't, and all that was lost was $500.

What if I spent $1000 or even $2000? If I even got one individual to invest $25,000 or $50,000, it would have been very much worth it. Research these email lists, and once you find a company, slow down. Let them sell you on the quality of their lists. Tell them you wish to talk to past clients. Be a hard sell, just like any investor will be.

Then, once you've made your decision, make sure your pitch page or your email pitch is freakin' perfect before sending it out!

Another idea for list building is to use a program called an email "Spider." This program will search the web, based on various strings such as "Dentist," and return monster lists of email addresses. Once again, you get what you pay for, and the top Spider software will always give you better quality results.

Trick #5: Find Any Connection

I once did a blast to a bunch of HNIs in Red Bank, New Jersey. Honestly, I can't remember how I found them. I believe it was through a friend who was in the printing business and had their names and addresses (but no email addresses). The connection here is that I was born in Red Bank. I formulated a letter that stated, in not so many words, that I was a hometown boy who was making movies and was looking for investors. I did a direct mail to over 200 people.

This time, I didn't turn up a single lead, but I've never believed direct mail to be an effective tool. If I had their email addresses, it might have been a different story. But that wouldn't stop me from doing it again. I never stop until the check's in the bank!

The crucial point here is that you must always be thinking about connections. How can you network? What's special in your life that you can connect to other people with? Was your father a police officer? Great. Go to a policeman's organization and show them how you are making a film that portrays law enforcement in a positive light. Look, this might not be the movie you want to make, but it could be the movie you are going to be able to get funded!

You Never Know Where Your Money Will Come From

Because your resource stream will be unpredictable, you have to be ready to adapt.

For example, I had written a four-page treatment for a horror movie, and I attached a director of incredible value (this project is still being developed, so I won't go into detail). The film was to be set in New Jersey in the Pine Barrens. In the meantime, I had recently read in *Variety* that Dubai was giving a lot of money to feature films.

I contacted (via email) an organization in Dubai, introduced myself, and sent them a link to my website, as well as a bio. Someone got back to me within two days, and was very interested in reading my treatment. They were truly excited, especially if the project could be shot in Dubai.

I hadn't thought of that! I just was looking for money! But what did I do? I rewrote the four-page treatment within a day and re-set the movie completely in Dubai. I'm still pursuing this financing, and you can check my websites to see if I can get it done.

One last tip: I once read HNIs listen to and trust their accountants more than anyone else. Think about it. An accountant is the person the HNI is already entrusting with his or her money. Find a way to get in with the accountant and you're golden.

I've already mentioned that, in preparation for a career in the film business, I read tons of industry-related books. A large percentage were books on sales techniques. You must consider yourself a salesperson. This is a business where the salespeople are now running the studios.

I never stop learning. My free time is spent reading books that relate to the industry, or fiction written by great writers like Elmore Leonard, so I can really analyze his work and raise the quality of my writing. The bottom line is, I consider it all work, even if it's fun for me. Never think you know everything! I'll pick up a sales book every once in a while and see if I can acquire up a tip or two. Appendix A lists a terrific title in this genre.

HNIs are out there. It's your job to find them by any means necessary. Perhaps you will be able to come up with some creative tricks that I haven't listed.

What's key is that you have to be able to adapt, because you never know where the funds will come from. Be ready.

STARTING THE TRAIN

8

Forget Stopping It!

Nothing is gained by approaching your quest for funding with anything less than 100% of your time, energy, and focus. You have to live, sleep, eat, and breathe that financial goal you have set for yourself. When I begin to raise money for a film, I call it "starting the train." I know that because a train is so powerful, nothing can stop it from reaching its destination.

That's the attitude you need to adopt. Your train will reach its destination. This chapter will go over the motivational techniques to get your train started.

First Dollar In

The "first dollar in" investment is the hardest to get, but it's the one that I most equate with starting the train. If you are able to land this, the train has begun to move and most likely will not stop.

Why is this investment the hardest? Because "first dollar in" is the riskiest investment. If you're trying to raise $2 million for a film and you have a person who can only put $200,000 into the project, that investor is likely to have a common concern: "What if you don't raise the rest of the money?" In other words, what happens to that person's investment if you can't raise the remaining $1.8 million?

Some people make deals where the money is committed via paper (don't trust a verbal commitment), or, even better, the money is placed in an escrow account for a certain time period. In this scenario, once you, as a filmmaker, are successful in raising the rest of the money, you will be allowed to start spending the $200,000.

I've been lucky and have not had those restrictions placed on the investments that I've been able raise. When you're developing a film, some money needs to be spent, no matter what. You may also want to spend a good portion of the money using the Attachment Approach (see Chapter 12: The Attachment Approach). Even if you don't use this method, however, a certain amount will always need to be spent, whether it goes toward plane tickets, AFM market passes, or dinners and lunches you have to pay for.

The investment of "first dollar in" is risky. The way to combat this is to pitch your HNI on the fact that you are "starting the train." His or her investment will be the catalyst for the film to go forward.

You may also want to give them extra incentives. First off, no matter what the amount of the first dollar investment is, give them executive producer credits! Let them know that, from that point on, the investments must be significantly higher for anyone to get that title.

Also, perhaps you may need to give the "first-dollar-in" investor a different percentage of the film, say, for example, a straight, undilutable 5%? This means that his or her 5% cannot go down, even if the budget of the film skyrockets. There are many creative ways to give incentives, which you may have to employ to land this most difficult investment. But always understand that if and when you get this investment, the train has started. You have to believe that you're on your way to making a movie.

Put It on Paper

The first and most important step to starting the train is getting your financial goal on paper. I don't mean on the business plan... you should already have that. I mean, if you're out to raise $2 million, take out a piece of paper and write in big letters:

I AM GOING TO RAISE $2 MILLION.

It's a great first step, but it's not enough. There's a phrase I hate, and it's "One day." People know not to say it around me. Things like, "One day I'd like to visit Europe..." or "One day I'd like to write a screenplay." "One day" rarely comes. "One day" is not definite. There's nothing in it. Your goals have to be specific. If you are saying to yourself, "One day I'd like to raise money for my film..." I can pretty much bet it's never going to happen. But, if you said to me, "I am going to raise $2 million by September," then I'd start to believe you. How much? $2 million? By when? September. Perfect.

Now go back to that piece of paper and write it loud and proud:

I AM GOING TO RAISE $2 MILLION BY
<INSERT DATE>

Then sign your name at the bottom. Something magical has already happened. This thought in your head has become tangible. You've taken a thought and made it into a real piece of matter that you can touch and feel.

The next step is to take that piece of paper and stick it where you will be able to see it all day, every day. Every time you look at it, remember your goal. I also recommend reading this goal to yourself in the mirror every morning. Why? Because while you're still half asleep, the goal will get embedded in your subconscious, and you will find a way. I'll go into much more detail on this in Chapter 15: The Law of Attraction.

This is an exciting time! You are not thinking about "One day." You are living in the now, and you are starting the train. Be psyched.

Obstacles

You need to pay the bills. Maybe you've got a job that's time-consuming. Maybe you work as a bartender, a hotel manager, or in information technology. Should this stop the train? No way. It's just an obstacle, and a moving train will run right through it. I mentioned those jobs because, prior to making a living in the film industry, I held all three at various times. But with each one, I was able to find ways to work in the film business.

As a bartender, I was able to talk to people and develop some fantastic characters. So many characters you see in my films are loosely based on personality traits I observed in the people I've served drinks to.

As a hotel manager, working the overnight shift for the Paramount Hotel, half a block from Times Square in New York City, I got so many crazy stories, I actually put them into a script for a film I'm developing.

As an IT (information technology) manager, having access to computers throughout the workday was a definite plus. I could search the Net for information, and build lists. I also had access to copiers, fax machines, and all those other devices I could use to print scripts and one-sheets, and make promotional materials.

That being said, I always did my job exceptionally, so, in all three I've listed, I would have easily been forgiven. I also made it clear to every place I've ever worked that I didn't want to be there, which always produced the strangest result. I got promoted so quickly. I guess every job thought that if they just threw money at me, I'd stay. I'd like to think this is because

I'm also a top-notch worker. You must maintain the belief that you're supporting yourself with this job just until you are able to work full time in film.

I am going to recommend something that may sound crazy. If you have any means to support yourself, quit your job. And don't just threaten to quit or plan to quit. That's not a commitment. I have a wannabe producer friend who has called me half a dozen times and said, "I'm quitting my job to-morrow so I can fully focus on the film business." Guess what? He's still working at that job.

Dr. Wayne Dyer has a brilliant take on this. He states that all decisions are instant. It's the decision to make a decision that takes so long! Think about it. All the people who have quit smoking take forever to decide to do it. When they actually quit, the act of choosing comes instantaneously.

You cannot get wet just by touching your toes in the wa-ter. You have to jump in the pool. Nothing is a better motivator than the need to make money. Some of the laziest people I know are also some of the richest, because they have nothing pushing them forward. I personally know that if I don't keep working in the film business, I could lose my house and not be able to send my kids to preschool. That's a damn good motivator.

If you must stay at your job, use it. Go back to the exam-ples of the jobs I worked. Make sure you take down character observations, or get free copies of your script, or do Internet work… anything. Just keep remembering that you are on a secret mission to make your film happen, and you need to continually work at it. There's a lot of fun and excitement to be had believing that.

Detours

The train may encounter detours en route to reaching its destination, but nothing is going to stop it. Let's take a look at some of the most common detours that, at first, are going to make you want to give up. If you stay the course and keep visualizing the train moving forward, you will get by.

Investor Pulls Out

This is so freakin' common, I almost expect it to happen. If someone told me, "100%, I'm investing in your movie!" I'd value that at around 20%. You never know what investors are thinking before they write the check (or wire the money). Maybe they ran into an old friend who said investing in film is a worthless deal. Maybe they lost money in the stock market. Or maybe, (and I've run into this several times), they're just full of shit and never had the money anyway. I'll never understand it, but I think some people want to pretend they have a lot to invest but really don't. This is a common problem. The key is, your train is moving forward, and you have to believe that someone else is going to jump onboard. What's great is that you already have the mindset that the film is happening, which will manifest someone else for you. Believe it.

Falling Victim to a Scam

Happened to me more than once. I told you about that organization that took $60,000 of my money (which I still have never seen). Some people would stop right there, but I did not. I just let it go and moved on with $60,000 less. As with the first problem (investor pullout), you may have a signed contract. But what are you going to do? Sue that person or entity? Again, suing is usually not an option. Courts are not quick! You will be tied up for most likely three years and have to pay legal fees up the wazoo. In fact, scam artists in the film industry count on this. They know you're not going to sue, because your goal is to get a film made, not sit in a courtroom. You just have to be careful when you're meeting new people, and try to qualify them as much as possible by asking around before you commit any funds or time. But, if you do get scammed, let it go and move on.

A way to avoid this is to have a "ring" of people that you go to when you need to qualify someone. If you're about to do business with a particular person or entity, make sure to contact everyone in your ring (which is comprised of industry people you trust), and see if they have worked with this person or entity in the past. It's a great way to use networking to find out if someone is legit. You will also want to Google the person or entity's name to see if there's anything on the Web about them. If there is, confront them. It doesn't mean you have to walk away. It's just a red flag. Ask them their side of the story, and, if it suffices, that's acceptable. But if you hear repeated stories about a particular person or entity, stay away!

Business Plan Changes

Okay, so you find out a person wants to invest, but he wants the film shot in Hawaii, and he wants the budget to be cut in half. Well, as we covered in Chapter 5: Creating the Business Plan, you better fire up your word processing software and start making changes. Be careful, though, not to go too crazy. Maybe your film definitely cannot be shot in Hawaii. Maybe you need that extra money. You have to weigh this against a bird in the hand. If this potential investor is real — a *true* HNI — what's this funding worth to you? Is it worth changing the whole script? It may very well be!

Keeping the Forward Momentum

There's magic that exists when you are "starting the train." You can feel yourself being swept up with the excitement that your film is going to be made! Nothing should deter you from this goal.

Don't disperse too much of your energy and excitement. Keep a certain amount inside, just for you. It's a great feeling.

Remember that deadlines can help. When are you shooting the film? What is your goal date? I love deadlines and use them all the time. How do you think I wrote this book? Sometimes, if I need a deadline on a script that has stalled for me, I'll make sure to create one. I will email a producer or distributor friend and tell him or her that I have this great new script. He or she will write back and ask, "When can I read it?" I respond that it will be ready in a week. Now I've just given myself a deadline!

Never, never, never give up. That's the best advice I can offer for starting the train. Persistence will pay off in the end. I've included a poem by a poet named Edgar Guest. I use it to close all of my motivational speeches to kids. It's about not giving up, and it's the attitude that you have to carry with you if you want to succeed in the film business.

Don't Quit

When things go wrong, as they sometimes will,
When the road you're trudging seems all uphill,
When the funds are low and the debts are high,
And you want to smile, but you have to sigh,
When fear is pressing you down a bit —
Rest if you must, but don't you quit!

Life is strange with its twists and turns,
As everyone of us sometimes learns,
And many a fellow has turned about
When they might have won, had they stuck it out.
Don't give up though the pace seems slow —
You may succeed with just one more blow.

Often the goal is nearer than it seems to be,
to a faint and faltering man.
Often the struggler has given up,
When he might have captured the victor's cup;
But he learned too late when the night came down,
How close he was to the golden crown!

Success is failure turned inside out!
The silver tint of the clouds of doubt.
And when you never can tell how close you are,
It might be near when it seems afar.
So stick to the fight when you are hardest hit!
It's when things seem worst that you must not quit!

Edgar A. Guest
(1881–1959)

THE TEN-ARM
APPROACH

9

My Bread and Butter

The Ten-Arm Approach is the bread and butter of how I raise money for films. I call it the Ten-Arm Approach because imagine a person with ten arms, each doing a different task. One may be talking on the phone, one may be typing an email, one could be doing research and building a list. Every arm is working toward achieving your financial goal.

Let's focus for a moment on your work ethic. If you think raising money for films is easy, think again. Why would I write a chapter entitled "What No One Else Can Do?" Raising money is a task that takes full-time work and effort. I firmly believe that a lot of people in the film business are just lazy. Scratch that, I firmly believe a lot of people in all walks of life are just lazy! Taking action is the only thing that separates the millionaires from the paupers. As we'll explore later in Chapter 17, you must take action!

Here's where the laziness comes in. Everyone wants the easy sale. They want to be able to make one phone call and get the money they need for their film. Trust me, I want that to happen too. I wish it were as easy as one phone call and one pitch. But HNIs with real liquidity want to hold on to their money. How do you think they got it in the first place?

At one point, while you may be looking at previous chapters (like Finding the Money), or looking ahead and reading new chapters, remember this. All of the elements and approaches should be used together to finance your film.

You cannot put all of your eggs in one basket. You must be able to use pieces of all the approaches, and continue to do so until your film is financed. I'm constantly making sure each approach, or each "arm," is being serviced, and I'm making progress and forward momentum with each. This is essential.

Don't Be Afraid to Tell People You Don't Need Them

When you're running concurrently on several HNIs or investor groups, you may have this irrational fear (it's common):

"What happens if party A gives me $2 million? What do I say to party B?"

Okay, first off, you should be so lucky. Second, as I said, it's completely irrational. Raising money always works in your favor. Success always works in your favor. When you go back to party B and say, "I got the money," they will most likely be relieved because investing money is a hard decision and they know there was a risk involved. After thanking them, you tell that party or that HNI that you will keep them in mind for the next project (or immediately start pitching them on another project). The key is, you've shown them success! Keep them in your database and remember them for next time. There's always going to be a part of them that wants in and feels they missed an opportunity, so your position with them has actually grown more powerful.

Continue on All Paths Until the Check Is in The Bank

I can't stress this enough. You cannot just buy an email list, get one lead, and say to yourself, "I'm done." You're setting yourself up for a monster failure.

Here's a technique that I practice. Let's say I'm setting up a deal for a $500,000 film. I've pitched an HNI and he commits verbally. Do I stop? Not a chance. I know there's a chance that he will pull out before that check is in the bank. So what do I do? I start to pitch everyone else even more aggressively. Now it's easier, because I also know I have someone lined up who's looking good. If I start pulling in a bunch of "noes," I can make changes and refinements. But it's always good to get word to your network that you're making more projects. And the pitches get easier once you have that air of success around you.

I also start to really amp up the other approaches. I take meetings with agencies, managers, and production companies. I've started the train, and it's moving, remember?

The best side effect of this method is that you might be able to 1) get a better deal (but always remember that a bird in the hand is worth two in the bush); or 2) get some other useful developments with the film because you are now funded.

Let's go back to the $500,000 film. Say I got someone to commit verbally, but the money still isn't in the bank. I would go out to several distributors and let them know that I have a funded film that's shooting in three months. Right away, they are going to be interested, because the money (the hardest part) is already there.

Now let's say I get a distributor to agree to distribute the film internationally. In the meantime, my investor pulls out. It sucks, but I deal with it. This is an all-too-common obstacle. The bonus is that now I can start pitching other HNIs because I have international distributors, so I've made my pitch more powerful. I keep stepping it up every time. Do you see how the Ten-Arm Approach works? If I had put all my eggs in one basket and just waited for the first HNI, I'd be back to square one. You must really practice the technique of propelling everything forward.

The best baseball team I have ever seen play were the 1998 Yankees. I had been a lifelong fan, and even rooted for them in the mid-eighties when they were consistently in middle to last place. Everything turned around in 1996 when they pulled off a World Series win over a superior team.

But 1998 was different. I have never seen a team like this, and perhaps I never will again. (Plus now I don't have time to watch baseball games!) They threatened to score almost every inning. They won more baseball games and achieved the best record in baseball history.

How does this relate to film? Well, here's what they would do, almost every inning:

- ◇ Someone would start off and get walked or get a base hit. (This is your initial HNI that you got involved.)

- ◇ Then someone would sacrifice-fly that person to second base. (This is you getting some foreign distribution or a packaging agent involved.)

- ◇ Perhaps at this point, someone would strike out, creating two outs. (This is your investor backing out.)

- ◇ Then someone would get a hit and drive that person from second base to home plate, and the Yankees would score. (This is you pitching other investors because you've advanced your project forward, and this is you scoring a sale.)

Every inning was a threat, and, even with their failures (strikeouts and pop flies), they were moving the project (scoring runs) forward. This is the science that you need to apply to advance your film. The Yankees wouldn't score every inning, and you won't score every sale, but you must always be pushing. Keep the train moving, and keep propelling it by adding value.

Don't Say You've Closed Until You've Closed

I've run into this problem countless times with other people. I learned this lesson very well on *The Attic*, when I believed a producer who told me he had closed $300,000. That $300,000 never came, and what happened? I did nothing while I was waiting for it. I sat there. Then, once I discovered that the $300,000 wasn't coming, I ran around like mad trying to raise the rest of the money, and ended up using the Dangerous Approach because we were already shooting.

Telling someone you've closed when you haven't evokes laziness. I've seen it happen the other way. On *The Alphabet Killer*, I told the other producers that my connection in Rochester was going to invest. What happened? No one did anything until my guy invested. Thankfully, I turned out to be right, but what if I had been wrong? The film would have fallen apart. As a producer, you have a responsibility to yourself (and perhaps your family) to maintain a healthy skepticism. Like I said, I pretty much consider every deal to be tentative until the money's in the bank.

Photo by Peter Gurin

Director Rob Schmidt gives me some tips before shooting a scene in The Alphabet Killer.

Telling someone you closed when you haven't is also a risky bet. This leads to other troubles that can be serious. A lesser consequence can be that you're considered the "Boy (or Girl) Who Cried Wolf," and people just start to think you're full of shit. The greater consequence can be that your producing partners move forward, make deals, and ultimately face lawsuits arising from contracts they executed because you said, "I've closed the money." Big mistake.

When I'm pitching investors now, I'm known for never giving anything away to my producing partners. I do not talk about the fact that I might be close to closing until I feel that I am one step away. It's very funny. You won't hear from me for a few weeks, and then, out of the blue, I will call and say, "I've got the money." I've done this more than a few times, while in the meantime, my producing partners would tout how they were taking meetings daily (and nothing would come out of these meetings). A lot of producers will take meetings with prospective investors who show interest, prompting them to tell everyone immediately, "The deal is done." Not only does that make you out to be the "Boy (or Girl) Who Cried Wolf," but also it could actually be dangerous (as I touched on above). As in the cases of *The Attic* and *Love N' Dancing*, believing in a few financiers other people had brought to the table almost sank both films. In both cases, I had to realize that the only solution was to take the bull by the horns and do it myself.

By the time I'm telling you, "I've got a guy," I've probably taken fifteen of those meetings where there was interest, and created fifteen different business plans. I normally don't tell other producers because I'm afraid they'll stop working… and they most likely will.

Everyone knows that when I say, "I've got a guy," there's a very good likelihood that the person I'm talking about is going to invest. In fact, I'm proud to say, at the time of this writing, my record is 100% when I've made that claim. There's just an instinct that I get when I know I'm going to close. I'm probably cursing myself by writing this (I'm trying to close a guy this upcoming week, and I've already told a few people, "He's in"), but I'm not worried. I'll always have a high percentage because I don't talk about my meetings!

Watch out, though. You don't want other people to think you aren't working. I fell victim to this once. A producing partner was taking all these meetings and talking trash about how he was the only one funding the film. Guess what happened? His big group of investors fell out, and we were screwed. Thankfully, a bridge loan company that I pitched came through for a few million. I didn't tell anyone about the bridge loan company until we were about a week away from closing.

Use It

Make each arm work as hard as the others. As you read about the approaches that fill the next group of chapters, keep in mind that versatility is critical. If you are having some luck with the Finder's Fee Approach, start really pushing the Distributor Approach. If you are getting ahead with the Distributor Approach, start pushing the Attachment Approach. The Dangerous Approach is the only one that should be used exclusively… it's a personal preference.

The key is to not give up and to be working every angle at all times. Constantly ask yourself, "What am I not doing that I should be doing?" This is the way your film will be financed.

Now, let's get to the specifics of the other approaches.

THE FINDER'S FEE APPROACH

10

Six Degrees of Separation

Have you heard the theory of Six Degrees of Separation? It goes like this: If I know you, I am one degree away from all the people you know, and two degrees away from all the people they know, and so on to the sixth degree. The Six Degrees of Separation theory states that no two humans on this planet are greater than six degrees away from each other.

Taking that into consideration, think of the remarkable amount of people you are two and three degrees away from! You have to believe that a good number of them are extremely rich, and at least one will want to put money into your film.

As stated in earlier chapters, money is out there. We live in an abundant universe. Start believing right now that you can make it happen and that your money is only a phone call or an email away.

The Associate Producer

The "associate producer" title may have many definitions. The title is given away a lot in the film business. At root, the associate producer is the person or persons who introduce the production company to the financing source.

Simply put, the Finder's Fee Approach involves getting an associate producer onboard to help you find the cash you need to make your dream a reality. This process will entail going out to everyone you know and giving them your pitch, continuing to move closer to your financial goal.

I use the Finder's Fee Approach as the primary way of finding HNIs. I don't think there's a better method to use. This is the most powerful way to find the check writers.

Remember: Give Them a Gift

So here's where the positive energy comes into play. Since you are in money-raising mode (see Chapter 8: Starting the Train), all of your actions should be directed toward funding your film. Every person you come in contact with should get this same exact pitch, whether via email, on the phone, or in person:

> "Hey, <insert (friend/acquaintance/random person you met in a bar) name here>, I'm producing this amazing film and I need to raise $3,000,000. Do you know anyone who might be interested in investing? I have a dynamite pitch. If you introduce me to them and they do invest, you'll get an associate producer credit and a 4% finder's fee! Think about it… If you find someone who wants to invest $3,000,000, I'll write you a $120,000 check just for making the connection!"

Pitch Analysis

Okay, let's break this down:

"Hey <insert (friend/acquaintance/random person you met in a bar) name here>"

You never know who has money ties or a person who can introduce you to money ties, and you never know where you will meet them. You can never know all the people your friends are one or two degrees away from. Think about it… it's virtually impossible. Do you have a spouse? Do you know every single person she knows from her entire life? Unless you've been dating since kindergarten, the answer is probably "no." The key is to go out to everyone, whether you think they know money people or not.

"I'm producing this amazing film…"

Make sure you let them know it is amazing. Remember… you've got to believe that your film will make money to be able to get other people to put their money in! You have something amazing to sell.

"…and I need to raise $3,000,000":

Always let them know the number right away… no beating around the bush. Be as clear and as upfront as possible.

You can easily get into a bad situation if this number changes. If it goes lower suddenly, a potential investor will think you are desperate. If it goes higher, a potential investor might think you are scamming them for more money. Plus, if you think, "Hey, this money is coming easy," you may be tempted to drive up the budget. Or if you think, "This money is not easy to raise," you may be tempted to drive down the budget. Either way, you could get into trouble because you've pitched your HNI on a certain number.

Another problem that arises is when a star shows interest and asks for a certain price. Let's say you've allotted $200,000 for your main lead character. This big action star named Tim Thompson wants to do the show, but requires $600,000. You will have to raise your budget by almost half a million dollars. You have to make sure Tim Thompson is worth it, and you have to make sure that your investors are cool with your changing the numbers (realize that their percentage in the film will go down).

"Do you know anyone who might be interested in investing?"

You're playing it cool, perhaps hoping for the "Great Side Effect" (explained later in this chapter).

"I have a dynamite pitch."

Your pitch has to be dynamite. Once it is, be proud of it. Let your friend know that if he or she makes the connection, you're not going to screw it up. Connections are a commodity, and no one wants to give them up knowing you're going to make the "connector" (your associate producer) look bad. You're going to go in there and knock it out of the park.

> **"If you introduce me to them and they do invest, you'll get an associate producer credit and a 4% finder's fee!"**

Give your friend the number right away so there's no confusion (which could lead to problems down the road). If he or she balks at it, offer a reminder that a 4% fee is the standard industry rate. (See: "Exceptions to the Rule" at the end of this chapter.)

> **"Think about it... if you find someone that wants to invest $3,000,000, I'll write you a $120,000 check just for making the connection!"**

You have to paint a picture showing how much money your friend will make ($120,000 in this case), and how easy that money will come. The phrase "just for making the connection" makes it sound like it's easy money... and it could very well be. All you're asking your friend to do is make the connection.

So there it is. Get used to saying it so it rolls off your tongue. As stated, the little pitch paragraph above can also very easily be used as a bulk email to all your friends and acquaintances, or a mail merge as described in Chapter 7: Finding the Money. I do these emails regularly with each project I am developing. I even have a mailing list on my *tommalloy.com* site, and I send them the emails too.

The key is to know and believe that you're presenting your friend, acquaintance, or that random person you met in a bar, with a gift. He or she could potentially get six figures just for making a phone call, and instantly become a part of the film business with an associate producer credit. What a deal! You are asking for something, yes, but you're returning an enormous amount of value.

Remember: Your friend/prospective associate producer doesn't have to be skilled in film pitching at all. Sometimes, a person in this position starts asking too many questions and I say, "Let me handle that." You have to be the salesperson. You don't want to rely on someone else to pitch your film. It's lazy and irresponsible. Others will never have your same passion, enthusiasm, and excitement for the project.

What's worse is that your prospective associate producer might misrepresent your film. Remember, it's your pitch... it's your baby. No one can do it better than you. The goal is to get a face-to-face meeting, or failing that, a phone call (which can be used to set up the face-to-face meeting). You have to put your message out to the world constantly. Don't get lazy. Let your friends connect you to the money sources, but you have to be the one pitching it.

A conflict arises when your prospective associate producer wants to keep money contacts close to him or her. You have to be careful and considerate of this. Just keep pushing for that face-to-face meeting. If it never happens, the HNI might not have been real in the first place. Remember, people love to pretend that they work in the film business. It gives them a feeling that they're cool and they're "in the club."

Also watch out for the "bait and switch." I've seen this happen several times. Your associate producer uses your project to get in good with an HNI, then suddenly switches out your project for his or her own. That's precisely why I keep telling to you stay away from people in the film business when you're looking for HNIs!

The Great Side Effect

I used the Finder's Fee Approach to obtain the first big money I ever landed. Did I have to pay a finder's fee? No! Why? Because the person I was approaching as a finder decided to invest himself.

I discovered this amazing outcome quite by accident. I didn't know this friend of mine had the money to fund a film. I was looking for $300,000 to fund 50% of my low-budget thriller *The Attic*. I approached this one friend because I knew he hung around a big-money crowd. He and his friends played high-stakes poker every Saturday night.

SIDE NOTE

Poker players are the best people to pursue. I'm not talking about professionals (though one of the most famous in the world wired $500,000 to a film I was producing because my producing partner at the time sold him on the subject matter). I'm referring to people who play Texas hold 'em all the time. They are gambling on a regular basis. Film investment is a gamble. Make the connection.

I got a meeting with my friend using the Finder's Fee Approach. I went in there and gave him the same electrifying pitch I would give to anyone, hoping he would call around and get some friends of his to invest. When I finished, he was staring at his desk, lost in thought. There was silence for a moment, and then he looked up and said, "Maybe I want to invest my own money into this." And he did! It was my first big money investor/True HNI. And I landed him by using this approach.

My pitch worked so well, this HNI felt he would be missing an opportunity if he didn't invest (and I truly believed he would have been, which must have translated). That's the great side effect of the Finder's Fee Approach. It's a non-confrontational strategy for getting your foot in the door. Use this same approach with the "Big Fish." If he or she is pitched well enough, an investment may arise.

If not, it's still not a problem, because you may still have him or her out there looking for money for you. And that was really the initial goal.

The Daisy Chain

As stated previously, 4% is the standard film finder's fee. Now, if person A knows person B, who knows Big Fish C, how do you divvy up the percentage? The logical way would be to give 2% to A and 2% to B. How is this fair? Well, you're asking A to introduce you to a Big Fish, but A doesn't have the connections and can't do it. However, A knows someone who does. That's why 2% is justifiable. You have to make sure, however, that A understands this. You can get into major trouble if you promise 4% to everyone, especially if person A is actually entity A, comprised of several people, or A knows B, who knows C, who knows D, the real Big Fish.

This actually happened to me once. A producer friend had two associates, and he thought they were all going to get 4%, executive producer credit, and back end points. Yikes! I hadn't even considered that because I figured this producer had enough knowledge of and experience in the film business to know that his request was insane! Let's suppose you promise four people finder's fees of 4%. That's 16% gone, right away. Your $3,000,000.00 becomes $2,580,000.00, which is a major difference. Luckily, I was able to find funding elsewhere using the Ten-Arm Approach discussed in Chapter 10.

Exceptions to the Rule

Let's say your friend calls you and says, "Hey, I've got this rich guy who may want to finance your film, but I want a 5% finder's fee and a co-producer credit." Are you going to say "no"? Probably not. There are always exceptions to the rule. Now, if that same friend said he wanted a 10% finder's fee, a producer credit (the single most powerful credit in film, followed by executive producer, then co-producer, then associate producer), and five points on the back end, it might be a different story. Many other factors come into play. Money can get expensive. How far are you from your deadline to get the money? Have you made commitments to any above-the-line talent? How desperate are you? Are you considering using the Dangerous Approach (see Chapter 13)?

Remember, the goal is to get your movie financed. If you made a $3,000,000 film and it made $30,000,000 and you came out with $0 because you gave away all of your back-end points, would you say that all is lost? Hell no! You just proved to the industry that you can make money. You'll be a hot commodity, and you'll be working in the business for a long time.

Don't Give Too Much Away, but Be Flexible

On the flip side of the coin, don't give away too much of your film and *never* give away too much of your power. Power and leverage are everything in the film business. I've seen several situations where people (myself included), due to wide-eyed naïveté and a huge desire to make their film happen, gave away every bit of power and leverage they had.

As I conveyed to you in my introduction, I met this unscrupulous producer I've referred to as The SP (Scum Producer) who claimed he was going to finance my film *AnySwing Goes*. I basically said, "Take my script. Take my

talent, my time, take anything. Just make my film happen."
Big mistake. He took everything! He took the script and tried
to make it his own, and tried to push me out of the picture
completely. Lesson learned. I cringe when I think of all the
time and effort I put into that film over a three-year period,
although I like to think that the lessons I learned were very
much worth it.

Chances are you may encounter someone like this (you may
already have). Don't let it get you down. As long as you stay
persistent and focused (keep the train going), and maintain the
ability to change your approach (with dynamic and flexible business plans and pitches), you'll win in the long run (by "collecting
the noes," if necessary). Remember what I said: The SP has not
worked again in the film industry, and I've reached a certain level
of success. That karma comes back around. If I saw him today,
I'd thank him, because his horrible practices armed me with
defenses for every future creep I would encounter.

SIDE NOTE

I've had young actors come up to me willing to give
away everything — their rights, time, energy, credits, and their
money — to get their films made. Don't do this! Most young
filmmakers are scared to ask for a credit. Be adamant! An extremely successful friend (he works in visual effects for film)
once told me, "There's no ladder in Hollywood." And he was
right. You have to just say and believe you are at the top, and
you will be if you can raise money.

I remember observing a sharp intern on the set of *Love
N' Dancing*, thinking he had a future as a producer. Yet, here
he was, a lowly (probably unpaid) intern, and here I was, the
writer, one of the lead actors, and a producer, theoretically in
charge of over a hundred people on the crew. Why was I in this

position? Because I raised the money, and then I said, "I am the producer." Remember the Golden Rule, "He who has the gold makes the rules." Get that gold, and you'll be in charge.

Which brings me to another very important point. You have to understand that money is the single most difficult and most important aspect of the film industry (see Chapter 3: What No One Else Can Do). When you raise the money, don't let anyone take the power from you. Even if your producing partner might have produced forty films, chances are he or she didn't raise money for a single one. That means you are more valuable. Don't forget that, and don't give away too much power!

The problem lies in the fact that people get way too caught up with credits and back-end percentages, because they all believe their movie is going to make millions and millions of dollars. I fought tooth and nail with that WBD (Wannabe Director) on *The Attic* for a 1% back-end difference. The film will most likely double its small budget at the end of its sales run, but, by that time, the 1% will have amounted to less than $2000. Worth it? Not at all. The legal costs and stress levels were far worse. Keep in mind that your goal is to make a film, not to sit around speculating about what your percentages are going to total. But you'll be truly amazed at the bickering that will arise once there's money on the table. If you make a successful film, you will work again, regardless of what your back-end percentage is worth.

Other Ways to Find Associate Producers

I know a friend who posted on IMDbPro (the fee-based version of IMDb that all the industry uses on a daily basis) and found some money. Another did a posting on *Mandy.com* and found some money. Now, with those two sites, you may have to alter the paragraph slightly, because you're dealing with film people who aren't going to go wide-eyed when you offer them a finder's fee. You may have to add that you have "major attachments," a "tight script," and an "experienced producer." Never lie... you can and will have all these if you follow the steps in this book.

Let's go back to the techniques I presented in Chapter 7: Finding the Money. As I explained, I've had some minor success using opt-in email marketing lists of high net worth investors. It's a paid service (usually $1000 is the minimum outlay), but that constitutes a blast to 10,000 investors. Using the Finder's Fee Approach, you may want to try blasting to these people not as investors, but as potential associate producers. That way, you're offering them a gift. You're telling them they will get X amount of dollars if they find an investor. Think of the amazing number of people you could potentially reach if you even had fifty of these ten thousand looking for investors for you.

The key here is that you are offering a gift via email. If you follow the steps of this book, your pitch will be so remarkable, it will speak for itself.

The approach will always be the same. Your pitch and your business plan might be the only elements that change (see Chapters 5 and 6).

You must look to expand your network continually. Go to networking events. Join community groups. Do whatever it takes to meet more people. Believe in the Six Degrees of Separation and know that it's merely a numbers game. Your financier is out there. Now you just have to find him or her. Remember to Get Outta Dodge. There's no better place to look for finders than outside the film business.

The Happy Check

When the money's in the bank, write the finder's fee check immediately. Do not wait! This situation caused me trouble a while ago. I wasn't the producer in charge of writing the checks, and I assumed one of my finders for *The Attic* had been paid. Not the case. I got an email months later threatening a lawsuit. We corrected the problem right away, but the friend-ship and the connection were gone. You have to give them instant gratification… so they'll want to do it again.

Remember, even if the 4% check is for a huge amount, who cares? Write it and put a big smile on your face. You've got your money to make your film. This check should be the happiest one you've ever written!

THE DISTRIBUTOR
APPROACH

11

Where's Your Film Going?

At the end of the day, if you're going to make any money for your investors, your film has to have distribution. Depending on the budget, your film may require theatrical distribution (which is very tough for indie films these days), or video distribution (under which I'm also including TV). I have not discovered anyone who has made his or her investors money via Internet- or self-distribution. I'm not saying those people aren't out there, or that's it's truly impossible, but, at this present time, those channels will not make your investors money for the types of films I'm discussing in this book.

The two forms of theatrical and video distribution are foreign and domestic. I almost always "split rights" when I'm working on independent films. This entails selling foreign and domestic rights separately, as opposed to selling your film to a company that takes "world rights."

I split rights not solely because there's more money to be made that way (but there usually is), but because the model I usually follow is to attach a foreign sales agent before I've finished with the film. I call this the "Distributor Approach."

Fitting It into the Sale

Let's just say I'm presenting two business plans to a prospective investor. The first is for a thriller with a few marketable stars and an experienced director. The second is for a thriller with a few marketable stars, an experienced director, and a "negative pickup deal" with Sony Home Video. (A "negative pickup" is when a studio agrees to purchase the movie from a producer/filmmaker for an agreed upon fixed sum at an agreed upon date in exchange for rights to distribute the picture.) The second one, in this instance, is stronger. Sony is a major studio and they are going to push a large amount of units. You are using the distributor as an avenue for risk management, which is a major factor in closing an investor.

There are positives and negatives associated with what the Distributor Approach will ultimately do for your film (which I will cover), so you have to decide yourself if it's a strategy you want to use. If the HNI needs to be sold on risk management, which most of them require, you should highly consider focusing on this approach. It's a tool to be used to make the investor feel more secure in his or her investment, by minimizing the risk that he or she has to take.

If I'm telling you that Sony has projected $4 million profit from the DVD sales of the thriller, and I'm asking you for $3 million to make the movie, that's a pretty good deal. I've taken your risk ($3 million) and countered it with a sales projection from one of the top five video distributors in the world (the others being, at the time of this publication, 20th Century Fox, Disney, Paramount, and Universal). While it's important for your HNI to know that nothing is guaranteed, his or her position is a whole lot safer under this approach.

A reputable foreign sales agent's projections are very valuable. I like attaching these foreign sales companies even more than a domestic distributor (read below: The Pluses and Minuses of Attaching a Distributor). If they project $2 million as a minimum from your $4 million film, that's telling the investor that this reputable foreign sales company, as a minimum, is projecting 50% of his or her investment will be returned. And the best part is, that's before a domestic sale! This 50% (remember, as a minimum) is not reliant on obtaining a domestic distributor. Now, if you use the Structured Approach (See Chapter 14: The Structured Approach), you have a financed film.

You have to make sure the investor understands that, and keep reminding him or her that if your foreign sales company does better than their minimum projections (which they most likely will), the investment is covered even more.

The Pluses and Minuses of Attaching a Distributor

The Pluses

When you have a domestic distributor or foreign sales agent behind you, you can be sure that your film will do *something*. It may go straight to video, and it may not make millions of dollars, but it will make some money. It's a bird in the hand.

If you've attached any of the major studios (Sony, Paramount, Universal, Fox, Disney), you're going to do well. Video distribution is a big boy's club. Those distributors have the "ins" with WalMart, a major player in the video market. As much as 60% of DVDs are sold through WalMart. (You make far less from video rentals through Blockbuster and Netflix than through video sales at WalMart, Best Buy, etc.) The powerful companies are able to get films on the racks and push them out into the hands of consumers.

There's also another benefit to attaching a distributor early: If they commit, they've committed! If your film turns out to be a test pattern (though you're probably not going get them to commit again), they have to follow through with whatever the contract stipulates.

There's an excitement when a movie is being shot. Re-member the "crack high" I mentioned? Anyone who's been on an indie film set knows and understands this. If you're shooting a killer script, everyone feels elated (except for the one pissed-off crew guy you can always count on to pop up). On set, everyone feels the energy and believes the film they are shooting is going to be huge. You may be able to parlay that into a studio deal. I had two different offers from domestic distributors on my film *The Attic* as we were shooting. My producing partners and I turned them down because we thought *The Attic* was going to be the next *Halloween*! That just goes to show how you feel on a movie set. In that case, we should have taken the deal.

Even distributors can get caught up in the excitement and think that the film you are shooting is going to be bigger than it will actually be. That's when to sign with them. Don't get a big head (like we did with *The Attic*), and think that you're going to do even better. Be realistic, take the deal, and be happy!

Photo by Peter Gurin

Eliza Dushku and I confront Bill Moseley in a scene from The Alphabet Killer *while the camera captures it all.*

I was about to make the same mistake with *The Alphabet Killer*. While shooting, we almost had a major distributor come in and offer to buy the film for $4 million outright. Since the budget was around $2 million, we would have almost doubled our investor's money and had a major distributor attached before we were even finished shooting. The producers were split on what to do. I know we all had delusions that *The Alphabet Killer* was going to sell for at least $10 million, but I started to think back about *The Attic*. If the distributor came through with the offer, I would have petitioned strongly to take it, and I would have been right. We did end up selling *The Alphabet Killer* and, at the end of the day, we may make more than $4 million for our investor. If we had taken the $4 million offer, however, my HNI would have been paid back on his investment in January 2007.

The Minuses

Attaching a domestic distributor beforehand is more likely a safer bet than not attaching one, but there are a few scenarios where it does not pay off.

If you are a beginning filmmaker, most of the distributors that you will be able to attach are very small, and I would recommend staying away from any of the unknowns. When I say "very small," I'm not referring to the smaller boutique distributors like Anchor Bay or Shoreline. I'm talking about the distributors (and there are many out there) that no one's ever heard of. I'm sorry, but saying your film is distributed by Jones Partners Distribution (I'm just creating a name here) just doesn't have the same ring as Paramount Pictures. It's amazing, though, how many times I have projects pitched to me that have distributors I've never heard of attached to them.

The problem arises when your film turns out to be great. What do you do if you find out you could have had a 3000-screen commitment from 20th Century Fox, but you have a straight-to-DVD release through Jones Partners? Look, I will admit that this is a rare scenario (though I bet you're all thinking, yeah, that's what would happen with my film), but it could happen. Even more likely, and perhaps worse, is when your little wannabe distributor becomes a middleman and sells it off to a real distributor that winds up taking a large part (or all) of your profits.

Here's a simple method for finding out if your distributor is anyone: Go to IMDbPro! Look up the company. Have you ever heard of any of the films they've distributed? If not, forget them! If you have, find out the numbers that were returned. I do not recommend asking the distributor for references, because they are just going to put you in touch with the producers who like them, speak well of them, and/or have had a positive experience.

I'd say a better route is to contact the producers of these films directly (again, finding contact info on IMDbPro or Google), and get their thoughts on the distributor. So far, every producer I've contacted for information has been more than happy to discuss the distributor (especially if he or she hates the distributor).

Producers sometimes find themselves in an "A-Team/B-Team" scenario with distributors, as though the producers are forces for good, and they (the distributors) are forces for evil. I even recall a producer friend who started working for a distribution company and sent an email to all of his friends stating that he had "joined the dark side."

Where to Find Them

Unless you want to fly to France in May and pay ridiculous amounts of money (the Cannes Market), the best place to find foreign sales agents is at the American Film Market (AFM) in November in Santa Monica. I attended my first AFM three years ago and said at that point that, as an Indiewood film-maker, I'd never miss the AFM again.

During the AFM, both the Loews Hotel and Le Merigot Hotel are taken over by foreign sales agents plugging the films that they have brought to the market. The hallways are filled with buyers and exhibitors.

The lobby of the Loews Hotel and the outdoor area are always filled as well, but *be careful*. Pretty much all the fringe and scam artists also hang out here. I make it a general rule to stay away from anyone who doesn't have a tag. People either have producer passes, buyer passes, or they have passes from a distribution company. These passes are tags hanging around their necks. It's very much like the VistaPrint business card rule, but on a larger scale. If the person can't afford to pay the $500 or so for the AFM pass, or doesn't have enough connections with distributors to get a distributor pass, there's a good chance that person might be just a hanger-on.

At the AFM, you can get guides that contain the contact information (and email addresses) of pretty much every distributor or sales agent in attendance. What a great tool! You can add this to your database.

I will say that the AFM isn't the deal-making mecca that it used to be. Buyers are getting more and more conservative, but, at this point in your fundraising efforts, that doesn't apply to you. What matters is your ability to find the sales agents, create relationships, and make deals with them to sell your film.

Now, if you can come to these distributors at the AFM with some financing, well, they're going to be eating out of your hand. Use the other approaches in this book to get a piece of equity, and you'll notice how many doors open up for you.

Let's say 123 Pictures signs on as your foreign sales agent. Perfect. Add that to the business plan right away. You now have another tool to use to sell an investor. But how do you get 123 Pictures to sign on in the first place?

Landing a Foreign Sales Agent

If you prepare yourself using all of the elements I've described in this book, especially in Chapters 4, 5, and 6, you'll have a great pitch for the foreign sales agent.

At the AFM, I usually go down the list and see whom I know at each company. I might have a fantastic connection: Perhaps an old friend is now the head of distribution for one of the companies. Or I may have a slight connection: We traded emails a few months ago on a different film project. Or I may have no connection, in which case I will walk into their room at the AFM and tell them I've heard wonderful things about their company.

Then you ask for a few minutes of their time and give them your "gift" like you would give to any HNI. Foreign sales agents can be sold just like an HNI. They may offer to pick up the film for foreign sales. They may offer to pick it up for foreign sales and give a little bit of an MG (minimum guarantee). Or, they may want to be producing partners with you and partially fund the film.

It's not a cakewalk for you to go to the AFM and land a foreign sales agent to fund your project. But, as previously stated, if you bring something with you, such as a piece of equity, your task is going to be a lot simpler.

Other Ways to Find Distributors

Both foreign and domestic distributors can be found fairly easily. There are sites on the Internet that offer email address databases including everyone who attended Cannes in the previous year. Some charge a monthly fee, and some charge a one-time fee for the list.

I have had great success just surfing the Net. I once found a list of distributors from a Latin film organization. It contained personal email addresses from about half of the biggest distribution companies in the world. It was a total score, and the information went right into the database.

You can also do your research on IMDbPro, or buy the *Hollywood Creative Directory*, which is a publication put out each year by the *Hollywood Reporter*.

The Distributor Approach mostly involves more than just emailing, though, if you want to achieve results with a legitimate company. This strategy can be essential for managing the risk for your HNI, which is an invaluable sell tool.

THE ATTACHMENT APPROACH

12

The Initial Hurdle

If I had to pick an approach that I thought was the most likely to get my film made, this would be the one. As we discussed in Chapter 9: The Ten-Arm Approach, you should never limit yourself to one sole strategy, but I believe this is the most powerful avenue for making your dream a reality.

Its only real liability is the initial hurdle, which is getting the "first dollar in" investment (I suggest using the Finder's Fee approach for that). As I mentioned in Chapter 8: Starting the Train, the first dollar is the toughest, but that piece of equity is essential.

Let's say you want to make a $3 million movie. The goal with this approach is to raise $200,000 as development money. Check out the following page for an example of a development funds breakdown for a fictitious movie called *The Green Monster.*

THE GREEN MONSTER

$200,000 investment:
- ◇ Legal: **$10,000** for retainer
- ◇ Producers: **$20,000** retainer
- ◇ Writing fees: **$5,000** script option fee
- ◇ Casting Director: **$10,000** retainer
- ◇ Development expenses: **$5000** (flights, shipping, meetings, calls)
- ◇ Funds for Cast Offers: **$100,000** (10% pay-or-play offers)
- ◇ Contingency Development Reserve: **$50,000**

> Investment goes to "Development" of the project.

> Investor will have priority in being reimbursed in an amount equal to one hundred and twenty five (125%) percent of his or her entire capital contribution to the Company. **Upon financing of the film, investor is immediately paid back his or her investment. Therefore, investor is secured upon financing of the film.**

> Investor receives EXECUTIVE PRODUCER credit. All future investors must invest at least $500,000 to get this credit. Investor also receives a percentage of the back end based upon the final budget.

> Eventual budget of the film is projected to be $3 million.

> After 125% recoupment, all profit is split 50% to investor(s) and 50% to production company, which includes the producers, the director, the writer, and the actors and actresses.

> Any film investment, according to Section 181 of the Jobs Creation Act passed in 2004, is allowed as a tax write-off.

Analysis of Development Funds Breakdown for The Green Monster

Let's start by breaking down the funds:

Legal

You'll need a lawyer to start preparing paperwork such as offering memorandums and operating agreements. You'll also need him or her to open the LLC and make sure that is all squared away.

Producers

You need to take a fee immediately at the beginning. If someone gives you any grief, remind them that financing the film has to be your number one focus and priority, and you can only do that full time if you are on the payroll.

Writing Fee

You'll need to option the script, even if you wrote it.

It took me a long time to figure out that Producer Tom, Writer Tom, and Actor Tom were three different people. In *The Attic*, I just took one blanket fee comparable to that received by the other producers. If you are performing multiple roles, you need to collect multiple paychecks. If I am producing the film and I wrote the script, those are two different paychecks. Just because the writer happens to be me doesn't mean there's a discount. If we had to go out and purchase a WGA script, we'd be paying the price. I actually made it easier, so there's no reason to be penalized for that. Bottom line is, you need to make sure all of your roles in the film are separate!

SIDE NOTE

Casting Director

Start right away and get a reputable casting director attached. This will make all the difference in the world once you are down to the smaller supporting roles. Make sure he or she has cast films you know and liked. You can do this research on IMDbPro. Casting directors can be closed doors to actors, and a lot of actors are afraid of them. But that's not the case for producers. If you start flashing the money around (remember, he who has the gold makes the rules), the doors open rather quickly. Much like foreign sales agents or distributors, casting directors will be easily accessible if you have a financed film. You're able to pay them, and they will provide a service.

Development Expenses

You need to have a reserve for this. Like it or not, "schmoozing" is part of raising money, and that could involve paying for drinks or dinner. This is a necessary expense! Don't abuse it, and make sure to keep all receipts. On the back of the receipt, write what the expense was for.

SIDE NOTE

Here's a litmus test my producer friend Isen taught me that I've always found to be true. If you're pitching an HNI on your film at dinner, and you have to pick up the check, the HNI is most likely not going to invest (and is most likely not an HNI). A dinner tab is nothing for a true HNI, and the hierarchy as to who pays for dinner states that the executive producer (which this person will eventually be) picks up the tab for the producer (though you should always make a reach for your wallet). Unfortunately, the producer picks up the tab for everyone else (though it's a write-off on the film). On the flip side of the coin, if the HNI picks up dinner, it's a very good sign. He or she is spending money on you and on the film.

Funds for cast offers

This is explained in detail later in this chapter under "Development Expenses Explained."

Now let's explore the other points:

Investment goes to "Development" of the project.

This $200,000 will be used as development funds for the project.

Investor will have priority in being reimbursed in an amount equal to one hundred and twenty five (125%) percent of his or her entire capital contribution to the Company. Upon financing of the film, investor is immediately paid back his investment. Therefore, investor is secured upon financing of the film.

We discussed the 125% return in the Chapter 5: Creating the Business Plans. It's really just a bonus on top of their initial investment so that they see money first. After the 125% is paid back, the investor gets the standard 50/50 split with the production company (which consists of the producers, the director, the writer, the actors, etc.). What's more important here is to note that you are going to return the $200,000 to the investor upon financing the film by adding development expenses to your budget. If you want to shoot a $3 million film, make it a $3.2 million film. The extra $200,000 that you raise will cover this investor's initial investment. That person will still keep his or her share of the film, and look forward to a 25% return.

It's a great selling point. Obviously the person putting up the $200,000 is at risk. But the risk expires once the film is financed (and that point, the rest of the investors have the risk). You could also secure this $200,000 with a tax rebate. On a $3 million film, let's say you shot in New Mexico, where the rebate is 25%, or $750,000. You can earmark $200,000 for your investor from that tax credit. That way, he or she knows that, once your film is financed, at the end of production, he or she is getting their investment paid back, and it's completely secure. Again, the only risk is that the film does not get financed.

Investor receives EXECUTIVE PRODUCER credit. All future investors must invest at least $500,000 to get this credit. Investor also receives a percentage of the back end based upon the final budget.

This is just another incentive to give to the "first dollar in" investor. It's icing on the cake. Some HNIs may care, while others won't at all. I've actually had HNIs tell me not to give them any credit in the film because they didn't want other people hounding them for money.

Eventual budget of the film is projected to be $3 million.

Make sure they know exactly what the budget is projected to be. The word "projected" is protection for you, but don't take liberties. I've already included stories of how this can balloon or deflate, and the problems such fluctuation can create.

After 125% recoupment, all profit is split 50% to investor(s) and 50% to production company, which includes the producers, the director, the writer, and the actors and actresses.

Again, this was discussed earlier, but it's important to include this so the HNI knows that he or she will still have a piece of the film even after his or her investment is paid back upon funding of the project or receiving the tax credit.

Any film investment, according to Section 181 of the Jobs Creation Act passed in 2004, is allowed as a tax write-off.

If necessary, you may have to present this information in a separate document, or include the FAQ sheet that I have inserted into the business plan.

Development Expenses for The Green Monster *Explained*

$100,000 goes to making "pay or play" offers to viable cast that will add value to the film. $50,000 will be kept in reserve if additional cast attachments are needed to make the project more alluring to investors.

Years ago, agents could be contacted with scripts for their clients. The agent would pass the script to the star client, and if the client liked the script, the agent would give a "letter of interest." Then the filmmaker would take that letter and try to raise money. If the filmmaker was unsuccessful (as he or she was, most of the time), the agent would have to go back to the star client, inform him or her that the project fell apart, and risk getting fired.

The agents got smart, and, nowadays, the big ones will not even read scripts for their star clients unless you are giving "pay-or-play" offers. Pay or play means that if you are offering a star $500,000 to play a role, and he or she accepts it, you owe that star $500,000, even if your film doesn't get made.

Due to the lack of projects resulting from the writers' strike of 2007, and the current financial times, some agents are now accepting 10% pay-or-play deals, which means that if you were to make a $500,000 offer, you would only need to put $50,000 in escrow, and that money would only be at risk if the actor accepted the part. At that point, you would be able to say that the star is attached to the project, and you would have a certain time frame in which to raise money for the film. This is the best way to get star attachments of value for your project, thereby transforming it into a commercially viable film that can be financed.

Only Attach People Who Will Help Finance Your Film

Filmmakers tend to get excited once they start making offers. The name of an actor who might have been your favorite TV sitcom star of the 1980s gets thrown into the hat. You'd be so excited to work with him and start up a friendship. Hold on for second. Is this person going to get your film financed?

One of the best ways to find out who's worth what is to talk to a foreign sales agent, who will be able to tell you if Christian Slater is more of a pull than Matthew Perry. This person will be your source for finding out who means what from a financing point of view. You may want to check with multiple foreign sales agents and look for trends.

The important exception here is if the HNI absolutely *loves* this actor. That means the HNI will fund based on that person being attached. At the end of the day, getting the HNI to open his or her checkbook is the number one priority.

Directors

I always believe the first step is to attach a director. I've been extremely successful in attaching directors who have all added value to my past three projects. Here are the steps I've followed to land these talented directors:

1) Make a list of films that are similar to yours or ones that you loved.

2) Go to IMDbPro and see if you can find personal contact information for directors of these films. If you can, send emails asking them to read your script. If you only get the agent or manager contact information, move on to step three.

3) Contact the DGA (*www.dga.org*) and request a copy of the DGA Membership Guide, and find the directors' names in there. Often, this book will contain their personal email address. You can also find this information on the DGA website, which has a searchable database of members. If you can't find contact information here, move on to step four.

4) Google the hell out of the directors' names and try to find a personal email addresses. Remember the Googling techniques we went over in Chapter 7: Finding the Money. If all else fails, go to step five.

5) Contact agents or managers (preferably managers, who are usually more approachable) and ask them if their director-clients would like to read your script. Be persistent until this gets accomplished.

With the pay-or-play offer money that you have, you can attach an experienced director to your project. Now it's time to start making offers to potential cast members.

Cast

The first step here is to shoot for the stars, but be semi-realistic. If you think you're going to get Tom Cruise for your $1 million indie feature, you're most likely shooting too high (although, as always, there are exceptions to this rule, especially if the star loved your killer script). So, to start, always go big, but not gigantic. You never know who's going to like it and jump on board.

The only problem is, you have to put a time limit on your offer. We had an offer out to Natalie Portman for a film I did. Her agent loved the script and was going to pass it on, but then we got a call that said Natalie wouldn't be able to read the script for two months. Would it have been worth it if she read the script and signed on? Perhaps. But, in this instance, we wanted to move forward. Offers can take a long time. Most of them are two-week offers, and most will come back as a "No." This is when you have to start being realistic and aim for a lower tier of star talent. A good casting director can help guide this for you.

I usually have spent the first month making offers to the superstars, and I try to get the casting director to put a one-week time limit on these offers. That way, I can get four offers out over the course of the month. After that first month, I have the casting director put together a more realistic list. Then we start making offers to those people.

As stated, I always show the list with which the casting director supplies me to a foreign sales agent so I can find out who means anything in the marketplace. Tip: I also run lists by investors. This gets them incredibly excited to see the names we're considering. I mentioned that sometimes the investor is taken by a certain actor or actress, so even if that person is not worth as much in a foreign market, you may want to make the offer to him or her, just to appease the investor. But even if an HNI is leaving it all up to you, he or she is still going to be excited to see a list of star names.

It's been my experience that when you get a bite from an actor or actress, you can almost always land him or her for the role. This has only failed me once, and it was because we didn't want to pay a ridiculous salary for a young female performer (who wanted almost $1 million, when our offer was $400,000). But every other time, when there was interest, I've been able to close.

Now that you've got your star (or two) and your director, you have the beginnings of a package. Perhaps you've spent $150,000 of the $200,000, but you've made your project a lot easier to finance. Now go back to the other approaches and start them over. Certain ones, such as the Distributor Approach, will be much easier.

You may also wish to approach one of the large agencies (listed in Appendix B), or management firms, and try to get them to aid in "packaging" the film. Just like everything else I've mentioned, this door flies open when there's financing or a piece of equity behind the project.

Raising that initial "first-dollar-in" is very tough, but the only risk to the investor is if the film does not get financed. As soon as the film is financed, that person is guaranteed repayment (by tax credit or by the financing of the film, as explained earlier). And remember, the investor's money (except for $50,000 covering fees) will only be spent if the star or director accepts the pay-or-play deal. Once they do, you have a package to sell!

THE DANGEROUS
APPROACH

13

Hang on for a Bumpy Ride

I remember hearing stories of Wall Street brokers who were just starting out. They would buy a Ferrari, knowing that they had to pay ridiculous amounts of money per month just to keep the car. Crazy? Yes. But, it was a way to motivate them to make the sales. If they wanted to keep their car and not get it taken from them, they found a way to get their commissions by working hard.

That's an example of a dangerous approach. There are no ifs, ands or buts… it's risky. But it works a lot of the time. I remember watching football games and seeing how most teams play their best when there are two minutes remaining and it's all on the line. I would say to myself, "If they just played that way the whole game…" Think of this and apply it to film financing. If you just played at your most intense level full time, what do you think you'd accomplish? For most people, it's hard to get this motivation. The dangerous approach provides it, no doubt.

The Pay-Or-Play Deal

We discussed aspects of the pay-or-play deal in the last chapter. Attachments are indescribably helpful in getting your film made. I'll relay a story of how you can combine the dangerous approach with the pay-or-play deal.

On the film *Love N' Dancing*, we had a $500,000 pay-or-play offer to Amy Smart. There was, of course, a due date on this money. If the film wasn't shooting by August, we owed her $500,000. Here was the problem: We only had about $600,000 in the bank! So if we didn't raise the minimum cost budget (which was $3 million, I believe), we'd lose five-sixths of our money and our star, and we'd be dead in the water. Talk about motivation. We (my producing partner at the time and I) were on the phone, in meetings, and making pitches 24/7.

Me, Billy Zane, and Amy Smart in a scene from Love N' Dancing.

That was dangerous! There was a good chance we could have lost a lot of our money. But we didn't. The danger of losing everything was a great motivator, and it's what caused us to win (although Chapter 1: Indiewood has already familiarized you with the other problems we faced on *Love N' Dancing*).

Many, many producers use the Dangerous Approach. Anyone who has watched an episode of HBO's *Entourage* knows that Jeremy Piven's Ari Gold uses the Dangerous Approach almost daily. It's what often drives this business.

Some people are crazy. They take action that borders on the illegal, or is, in actuality, illegal. In the previous story about the pay-or-play deal, nothing was illegal; it was just risky to our initial investor. There were no qualifications put on the money we had already raised.

In some situations, though, producers will promise money that's not there. I heard a story of a guy who made something like five pay-or-play deals to big stars, but didn't have any financing. Once he had the stars, however, he had a package to sell. (And, from the story I heard, he did it.) But that constitutes fraud, and it's illegal. If the guy hadn't raised financing for the film, not only could he have been sued or even gone to jail, but his reputation in this town also might have been destroyed.

Deadlines

It's all about motivation. Giving yourself a personal deadline to raise money for a film is a great motivator. But if you also start spending money, whether it be your own, development funds, or initial investments, it could become dangerous.

I've told you earlier how I sometimes create deadlines for myself to give me personal motivation. Even if you procrastinate, the deadline still has to be met. The reason so many people have films in development for years (or for eternity) is that they haven't given themselves a deadline to raise the money. They are using the "one day" approach. "One day I'm gonna raise money and shoot my film." Never gonna happen. *One day never comes.*

But for some people, it's just not enough to say:

> "I'm going to raise the full budget of my film by May of this year."

They still won't do it. So they use the Dangerous Approach, and put the proverbial gun to their head:

> "I'm going to raise the full budget of my film by May of this year, or I've lost all the money that I've raised so far, lost my star commitments, and might end up losing my house."

Let's say two different people said those two different lines. Who do you think is going to try harder to raise the money?

Mind you, I'm not suggesting that you make crazy deals, live on the edge, and force yourself to raise money. This is called the "Dangerous Approach" for a reason. I've been there, and I've done it. It's not fun. It will give you gray hairs. But, for better or worse, it works.

The Best Time to Raise Money

I touched on this in Chapter 1: Welcome to Indiewood. There is, unfortunately, no better time to raise money than when you are shooting a film. When a film is in production, there's magic in the air. You can feel the energy. It's the "crack high."

Twice, I've been faced with the dilemma of raising additional money while I was in production on a film (*The Attic* and *Love N' Dancing*). On *The Attic*, I was able to help and pull it off. This was chiefly because I was only a supporting actor, and I had a lot of days off to focus on raising money.

In *The Attic*, I played the autistic brother of Emma (played by Elisabeth Moss, now one of the leads on TV's *Mad Men*). As Frankie, I was a soft-spoken, lovable guy, and that's all Elisabeth knew me as. One day I was on set in full producer mode, pitching HNIs on investing in the film to be able to complete it. After they left, I ran into Elisabeth outside the house and she admitted she almost didn't recognize me! She said, "You're a lot different when you're Producer Tom." She went on about how she was a little scared of me and liked quiet Frankie slightly better.

With *Love N' Dancing*, I played the lead role, so I was acting every day. If this is something you choose to do, you cannot be worried about anything else except your acting performance. I had to give over the other tasks to my producing partners, and hoped and prayed that they got the job done.

At no other time would we have gotten people to open up their pockets and give the money that they did to keep the film going as we waited for that big hedge fund (that never came to the table). The people who did invest were on set seeing the trailers, mingling with movie stars, and believing that they were film producers (which they were).

Talk about desperation from a producer's standpoint! I give a lot of credit to Robert Royston and his sister-in-law, Melissa McDonald, who was a co-producer of the film. When I first met them, they didn't even know what a film producer actually did. I made them both read *From Reel to Deal*, and, to some extent, taught them a lot about pitching investors. By the time the film was over, they were pros. I don't fault them for not closing the big hedge fund (I fault the liars at the hedge fund). They definitely pulled some deals in from out of nowhere that allowed the film to get shot. And they did it without my help.

I can't explain it, but somehow, when an independent film is shooting, you're kicked into high gear. Everything in your life becomes more focused and you handle problems differently. I imagine if you've produced an indie film, you're nodding in agreement right now.

So, if you take that heightened focus and mix it with a little desperation, you've got a man or woman on a mission. It's dangerous, but I've rarely seen a movie fail when all is on the line.

THE STRUCTURED APPROACH

14

Piece by Piece

A film can be built like a house. You can start with the foundation (a piece of equity), move on to framing (attachments), then go to exterior finishing (tax incentive), and finally end with interior finishing (finishing funds). Each of those steps can be tackled one at a time, as opposed to plopping down one lump sum and saying, "Give me a house."

Of course, when we're dealing with film finance, we'd love someone to plop down a lump sum, but if that's not going to happen, there are other ways to get your film financed. That's where the Structured Approach comes into play.

The Structured Approach involves adding pieces together to get an end product. Here's a little breakdown to illustrate how this works:

THE BIG FILM
$4 million budget

NEED:

1. $600,000 equity from a high net worth individual (HNI).
2. $1,200,000 derived from Michigan Tax rebate (40%).
3. $300,000 derived from deferred salaries.
4. $300,000 derived from postproduction deals.
5. $1,600,000 Minimum Guarantee from foreign sales.

Analysis of *The Big Film's* Structured Approach
This is an example of how to structure a movie's finances.
I'll go through each step, one by one.

$600,000 equity from a high net-worth individual (HNI).

Okay, no matter what, you always need a piece of equity. It's part of making a film, and if you try to go forward without it, you'll soon realize that you have nothing behind your project and it's going to fall apart. So use the other techniques in this book to find a piece of equity. Think about it, though. You're doing a $4 million movie, and I'm telling you that you only have to find $600,000, which is 15%! This is the incredible bonus of the Structured Approach, and what makes it so powerful.

$1,200,000 derived from Michigan Tax rebate (40%).

I picked the Michigan tax rebate, because, at the time of this writing, it is the highest. The thing is, to successfully use that money to make your film, you can't wait to get it from the state. Those tax rebates usually come ninety days after shooting. The only time I've seen someone wait for them is if he or she has shot the film and held off on postproduction, with the intention of using the tax credit to fund post. This only seems to work with smaller tax credits, because post is maybe 15-20% of the budget. In this case, to use the money up front, you would need to find a company that would cash-flow the tax credit. Of course, you're going to have to pay a fee. Also, since you're deferring some payments and are going to get a postproduction deal, the tax credit will be lowered because that money will not be spent in the state. NOTE: I chose $1.2 million because I calculated 40% of $3.4 million ($4 million minus $600,000 ($300,000 in deferrals, $300,000 in post deals), and I also subtracted $160,000 for fees that you would pay to get it cash-flowed.

$300,000 derived from deferred salaries.

This is a good incentive for investors, because it shows them that you have skin in the game. I would never suggest deferring all of your salary. But, if you can defer 30%, and use your best sales techniques to get the writer, director, and maybe a few actors to defer 20% or so, there can be some monster savings here. The only caveat is that if you don't spend the money, you won't get the tax rebate, so you must make sure the funds you are saving are more than the rebate money you'd receive with no deferrals. Remember to work into the contract that as soon as the film starts showing profit, these deferrals come out in first position, before anything else.

$300,000 derived from postproduction deals.

Postproduction facilities want the work. You'll need to speak to as many post facilities as you can and find one to make a deal with you for a certain amount of work. For instance, let's say there was $800,000 to be done on your $4 million movie. If you told a postproduction house that you would give them $500,000 for that amount of work, and offer them a share of producer points in the movie, it might be a great incentive for them. Some businesses are so excited and desperate to get the job that you may not even need to offer them the investor points. Again, same caveat as the deferred salaries. You will not be spending the money, so you will not be getting it back as a rebate. Make sure that the postproduction facility is doing $800,000 worth of work.

$1,600,000 Minimum Guarantee (MG) from foreign sales.

Here's where the Distributor Approach must come into play. You need to be able to bring a reputable foreign sales team to the table to sell your film. Certain sales agents, such as Voltage Pictures, who I used for *Love N' Dancing* and can't say enough nice things about, are so reputable, you can actually bank their numbers. What does this mean? When a foreign sales agent gives you sales projections, the document will feature three columns, based on what they believe they can sell the movie for: high, medium, and low estimates. You may be able to take the low estimates and get a bank loan for the rest of that money. So, for our $4 million film, we're stating that a reputable sales agent said he would be able to sell $1.6 million as a low estimate. This is a pretty big figure to qualify for the "low" column on a $4 million film, but we're assuming you've used the other approaches in this book and put some attachments together.

And there you have it. Your $600,000 has become a $4 million movie.

What happens if one of those numbers is lower? You can start shifting things around and playing with the numbers. Maybe your deferrals need to be raised, or your postproduction deal needs to be better. You're also going to need to get the money off of those foreign sales estimates.

Finishing Funds and Gap Financing

Finishing funds and gap financing are loans given by a bank or a funding entity that cover the missing money needed to finish a film. These loans are the first to be paid off when the initial money is returned on a film, and they usually come with high interest rates. I've dealt with both of these outlets before, and it's what I call "expensive money."

But it might be the only way to complete the budget of your film. Most often, these loans require some collateral, whether it is the tax rebate, the foreign sales estimates, or both.

For *Love N' Dancing*, the bridge lender, Cold Fusion Media, loaned us the money against Voltage's sales projections (minimum column) and the tax rebate from New Mexico (25%). They then gave us a 1.5:1 pull-down ratio on the loan, which means that because our sales projections and tax credit added up to $3 million, they loaned us $2 million (roughly). In this case, their money was incredibly secure. The tax rebate was guaranteed, and it would have been unheard of for Voltage to fail to hit their minimum numbers.

Quite a few companies around town provide gap financing, or even super gap financing (affecting a larger percentage of the film's budget). You have to research them via IMDbPro and *Variety* and start creating relationships there.

These days, banks are not loaning to films like they have in the past. I've never had success in getting a bank loan for my films. The collateral they require is just too great. Perhaps you know someone who would put up a personal guarantee on a loan, and you can get that person to facilitate your funding.

I almost was able to pull this off for a multi-million transaction. The HNI was going to get a huge check (almost $1 million) just for putting up a guarantee so the bank would loan us $5 million. The risk to the HNI would have been that we might not pay off the bank loan. But, if we did pay it off, he would have gained almost $1 million for literally doing nothing.

These kinds of scenarios start to get hairy and complicated, and they are extremely tough to pull off — but perhaps you'll have better luck than I've had. There's no reason not to try to go forward with it under your Ten-Arm Approach philosophy.

What's the Alternative?

What if you can't get a bank loan or finishing funds? Well, you can pitch an HNI on the foreign sales estimates. Those numbers may work just as well for your HNI as they would have worked for a bank or a gap financier. Think of your HNI as a bridge lender instead of an equity investor and pitch him or her that way.

If all else fails, lower the budget. If you have four out of the five elements you need but you still can't make that $4 million movie, make a $3 million movie! Remember, from Chapter 5, the MCB (Minimum Cost Budget) has to come into play. You have to be willing and able to do this. Would you rather not make a movie at all? Hell, no!

A Word of Caution

You must become a bit of a math wizard to use this method effectively. I'm always designing new formulas to try to structure a film and secure the investor's risk. It's fun to put together a scenario like this. In my limited free time, if I'm scribbling on a pad, you can almost bet that I'm trying to structure financing for a film. One day, I know I'm going to find the perfect formula!

But this can be a difficult method to pull off because you are not just trying to land one deal, but several. Just remember, though, the benefits of this approach are that you only have to raise 15% to 25% of the money you would have needed to raise for the entire budget.

If your "train is moving," and you have a "first-dollar-in" investment, structuring the financing might be the most logical way to go.

A final warning (I've been pitched about twenty times on the following type of deal, and I've even fallen for it a couple times): Place a certain percentage in the bank, say 20-30%, and, within a month or two, a certain entity will make the remaining 60-70% appear. Use logic here, folks. If you could place money in an account and have more money magically appear, wouldn't people be doing that all the time in endeavors other than film? Any seasoned financier will tell you these deals never close. Stay away.

THE LAW OF ATTRACTION

15

The Hot Topic

The law of attraction has become the hot topic as of late, mainly because of the book *The Secret*. The law of attraction is one of the most powerful forces in the universe. People's thoughts (both conscious and unconscious) create their reality. Basically, if you want something and think you can get it, it will happen. Similarly, if you don't want something, and think you will get it, it will happen.

We all have that friend who says, "I have the worst luck ever." Well, guess what? That's all he or she will attract. But if you say all the time, "I'm really good at cooking," well, that's going to come true as well. Reality is created by thought.

Right now, say out loud, "I'm great at raising money for feature films!" Believe it.

Knowledge of the law of attraction has been around for centuries. The book *Think and Grow Rich* by Napoleon Hill was written in 1937 and contains a philosophy quite similar to that of *The Secret* (except *Think and Grow Rich* focuses on money). I'd also recommend *The Power of Intent*, by Dr. Wayne Dyer.

Can I explain how the law of attraction operates? I could try. But I'm not sure that's even necessary. All I know is that it works. I've used the law of attraction consciously and subconsciously for every film I've ever produced. I take the basic principles and hit them with a shot of lightning, resulting in a method I've created that's like *The Secret* on steroids. Try it if you'd like, but be careful! There are dangers with this approach. It works for me, but may not work for you. Read on at your own risk.

Programmed Obsession

I call my law-of-attraction-based method "programmed obsession." It involves training your mind to focus only on your single goal. In this case, let's say it's "raising $3 million." Remember, as we touched on in Chapter 8: Starting the Train, that goal has to be specific.

Programmed obsession is basically forcing your mind to project only what you want, thereby giving a powerful push to the law of attraction.

The Secret advises you to think about what you want, ask for it, and then just wait for it to come. Not for me. I don't believe that fully works. Programmed obsession is the law of attraction customized for go-getters and hustlers. As Abraham Lincoln said, "Good things come to those who wait, but only what's left over from those who hustle."

Meditation and hypnosis are good at times, but they fade as your mind grows active. What if you could program your mind to see only your main goal? Then, all your energy would be focused on what you want (for better or worse).

Again, this method may not work for everyone. But it helps me tremendously. Try it and see what happens. You might just get your film funded.

Steps to Programmed Obsession

Let's start with this goal: You want $3 million to make your feature film, and you want it within two months.

First, lie on your back and close your eyes. Think of the end result — how you will feel when you have that check in your hands. Picture it! Picture yourself getting ready for pre-production. Picture yourself shooting the film. This should all make you very, very happy. Let that happiness flood through your body. You have raised $3 million for your feature film! It's happening! Force it so that it's the only thought in your head. How great do you feel right now? You've done what no one else can do. You've raised money for your film. You did it.

This process is called "flooding." It must give you that electricity!

As you are flooding your brain with these thoughts, you must feel it in your entire body. Squirm on the bed. Feel it actually flood your brain. Feel it seeping into your subconscious (which, if you do it right, it will).

It's best to do this around bedtime. If you fall asleep as you are flooding, that's no problem. It will aid in letting the goal into your subconscious. Go to sleep with a smile on your face. When you wake up, repeat the process again when you are still in half-sleep. It will be embedded in your mind.

You are filling your brain with positive energy and excitement. You can recharge this daily if you have to. You don't have to do the full bed-squirming flooding, but you should take a few moments to feel it taking over your brain. If you do, however, feel like you've lost your focus a few days or weeks later, repeat the flooding process as much as necessary.

Photo by Neil Jacobs

Dancing with Amy Smart in a scene from Love N' Dancing. *Notice the hearing aids!*

Now, here's the second part, and it's just as essential. You need to articulate your goal into every mirror or reflection you walk by during the day. If you are going to the bathroom, as you are washing your hands, gaze up into the mirror, look yourself in the eye and say, "I will raise $3 million for my feature film within two months." Feel that positive flow. Smile and be happy.

Do the same thing if you see your reflection in a computer monitor or a car's rearview mirror. Wherever you see your reflection, recite your phrase.

Your brain will be consistently and eternally focused on your goal. Your goal is this fantastic piece of music that's playing in the back of your mind. And it will be there, making you happy, until it's fulfilled.

Using this method, you have moved your mind into an active manifesting state. The key is, this goal must be life-encompassing.

Now you have to take action.

Each day, every step you take has to be focused somewhat on your goal. Remember what I described in Chapter 8: Starting the Train? If you work a computer job, start researching aspects of your project. If you work in a restaurant, start analyzing diners to see if they possess character traits you might want to add to your writing, performance, or direction, depending on whatever your eventual role in the film might be.

Let's face it, if you used the law of attraction, yet adamantly refused to take any steps toward making your film happen, it probably wouldn't work. But if you allow your actions to reflect your thoughts, then the positive focus you've applied will manifest your film.

So start planning for the movie! Take the steps as if the $3 million is already there. Tell everyone you know that you're making a movie two months from today. Carry out every action as though you're certain to reach your goal.

Everything depends on how often you flood and how effective your flooding is. If it fades from your mind daily, it's not effective. Push harder. Your mind must be completely immersed in the process.

After You Reach Your Goal

When you've got that $3 million check, celebrate with a gift from yourself, give a gift to someone else, or open a nice bottle of champagne. You did it.

Then take care of yourself. Get a massage. Relax. Meditate. Take baths. Practice breathing. Think of programmed obsession as if you were running a car at 200 mph. The engine is going to be hot as hell and needs to cool down. Your brain, which you've flooded so that you can achieve your goal, needs a cool-down as well.

It's very easy to get sick if you don't cool down after this method. Trust me, it happened to me about ten times. So, relax. Ease out of it. Then do a quick pat on your back and get going. It's time to focus on making your film.

GETTING
IT DONE

16

Back to the Crack

Just the other night, I closed a guy for $4.5 million. It was a great feeling… one of the best I ever had.

I had personally set up a screening room for this HNI in Hollywood through some connections, and he watched the film while I paced outside. Afterwards, he coolly said that he was impressed, and that we'd meet up for dinner. Going into dinner, I truthfully didn't know if he would close or not.

We met at The Ivy, along with my producing partner, Robert Royston, and actress Amy Smart (who had graciously donated her time in support of the film).

We gave the HNI the pitch we'd been giving on *Love N' Dancing* for over two years, and he bought into it. He felt our passion and our honesty, which is so key. As I've discussed in this book so many times: You have to believe your project will succeed! This HNI was a great guy, and he was also savvy. He knew he was getting into business with the right people.

That night, this HNI took us out to an exclusive club and was buying Louis Roederer Cristal champagne like it was club soda. He must have bought twenty bottles, and the club was most likely charging him $500 a piece. As I was toasting with him, I remembered two things:

◊ This feeling, though freakin' awesome, is merely the crack high.

◊ As fun as this is, remember that *this is work*.

Let me explain. Those nights that I just described rarely exist in Indiewood. Maybe they're a regular part of the Hollywood culture, but the Indiewood scene is all about hard work and stress. Those glory moments come few and far between, and you have to savor them when they appear. But if you think that's what moviemaking in Indiewood is about, you're in for a disappointment.

Most of my non-immediate family (cousins, aunts and uncles) think I live the good life, and to some extent, I do. I have a great house, a fantastic wife, and two perfect kids (the cutest kids ever). But these relatives also think I don't work.

As I've written earlier, I have worked other jobs. I was the I/T Manager for several companies. I was a hotel manager. I've been a consultant, a web designer, and worked in restaurants.

Nothing that I have ever done even remotely compares to the pressure and hours of the indie film business. I wish I could work an eight-hour day. That would be such a relief! But it's never that. A typical day: I wake up at 6:30 a.m. and help my wife with the kids. Then, by 7:00 a.m. I'm returning emails and calling people on the East Coast, where it's 10:00 a.m. That work, along with writing, conference calls, and collecting lists and information, goes until around 7 p.m., when I break for dinner (I eat lunch and breakfast at my desk). So there's twelve hours right there. Then I play with the kids and help put them to sleep, and resume working at 9 p.m. If I have to write or make lists, I'll do that until 11:30 p.m. or so, until I decide to go to sleep. So, that's a 14.5-hour day at minimum. If I have to go out and network and schmooze, I'm usually out until at least midnight, but most likely 2 a.m. So, when I go to sleep at 2:30 a.m., I've been working 17.5 hours. These days are not uncommon.

If you're getting into Indiewood for the glamour, go home. It only comes in tiny, fleeting flashes.

But if you're in it to work your ass off and make movies, you can do it.

One example I love to use to show people's perception of the film business relates to acting. When I do a motivational speech and, in the Q&A period, someone asks me about acting, I always bring up the hard work. Here's the story I relate:

At the top levels, who brings in more money, a doctor or an actor? There's no comparison. A top surgeon might make $500,000 a year. A top actor can make that in a month (or even a week). If I asked you how long it would take to become a doctor, you'd say that you'd have to go to med school, do an internship, and really commit. At minimum, it takes around ten to twelve years to become a top surgeon, and that's if you're lucky. Yet, for some wacky reason, people think they can make it in Hollywood or Indiewood in just a matter of months. You know how many times I've heard, "I gave the acting thing a try for six months, but I didn't think it was working out"? Do you think you would ever hear, "I gave the doctor thing a try for six months, but it wasn't working out"? Ridiculous!

The problem is, the exceptions to the rule are what always get publicized. Everyone knows Cameron Diaz was "discovered" at an open casting call. Everyone wants to hear the easy way out. I was "discovered" fourteen years ago at a restaurant in Little Italy. It's now taken me all those years to scratch the surface as an actor. But I'm committed for life. I always knew that. There was nothing else for me. I always used to say that I'd keep going until I was having a nurse push my wheelchair into an audition. With no teeth left, I'd exclaim, "I'm going to be a big star."

How do you feel? Do you have the fire? Will you never give up? That's what you need to make it in this brutal business.

People drop out of the film business all the time and they're forgotten. Actors and actresses move out of Los Angeles, get married, have kids, and get stuck in normal jobs. Directors, producers, and writers all do the same thing on a daily basis.

Will you be one of those people who gives in to the pressure? Or will you come out on top?

Some Tips

These are my last and perhaps most important lessons I can give to you. Some are random thoughts. Some are codes to live by. Let's assume you've lined up an HNI. He's worth over $200 million, and you need him to close your $5 million goal. This guy's a check writer, and you've already qualified him. Here are some of my best closing tips (in random order):

◇ Let him talk about himself. Don't just pitch everything about you, you, you! Ask him his story first. People love to talk about themselves!

◇ *Be energetic and passionate*! I can't stress this enough.

◇ If he is drinking, drink. If you're against alcohol, so be it. But know that you've just told your investor, subconsciously, that you do not share common ground with him. It's an obstacle. The same goes for the other way. If the investor doesn't drink, *do not drink*! I don't care if you're a raging party animal. Do not touch the stuff around him. If the investor is a drinker, you must not get drunk at any cost. If you are a lightweight, make sure you milk that drink all night. You always have to be ready to slip into business mode.

◇ Find common territory to talk about. I like to educate myself constantly and broadly by reading on a daily basis. This way, I at least know something about most topics an investor will bring up. If I encounter something unfamiliar in a meeting, I will research it so I have an advantage the next time. If an HNI brings up cars and I'm not really a car buff, what do you think I will be Googling that night?

◇ Google the person's name before you meet him. You might be able to find out something about him in a newspaper article that was published online. This will come in handy when you need to occupy common ground with him.

◇ Don't tell him you've closed (with a different investor) unless you've actually closed. I spoke about this earlier when I referred to not telling producing partners that the deal was closed. It's equally important to refrain from telling an investor you have closed with someone else until you have the money in the bank. What if your other investor falls through? You just lost your opportunity with this HNI, and believe me, he won't graciously give you another shot. I once had a foolish friend who thought it was a good strategy to tell this one HNI that we had raised financing somewhere else. You know what the HNI said? "Great!" And that was the last time we saw or heard from him again.

◇ Don't beat your investor in any card game, especially poker. This may sound stupid, but I once reamed out a producing partner for beating my HNI in a poker game and then talking shit about it. Do you like to lose? How does it make you feel when someone beats you and takes your money, and, on top of that, might be arrogant about it? Now, think of that feeling. Is that something you want an investor to feel?

◇ Don't ever brag about how easy it was for you to close other financing. This sounds like it would be obvious, but I've seen producers who lacked common sense do it several times. I even heard a story of a producer friend who went into a meeting with a group of HNIs and boasted about how he used to make money on the stock market by selling people stocks, collecting his money, and then watching the stock go to $0. Have some common sense, for the love of God!

◇ Always remember that this is work. If an investor calls you and asks you to go to the dance club with him or her, be ready to go at anytime… and be ready to *work*. Smiling and laughing and making jokes is all work, folks. Trust me… get really good at closing sales and you'll find this to be true. You have to set up a positive environment in which the investor will feel comfortable. The best way to do this is to be *fun*! But always be ready to slip back into business mode, and always be ready to work.

Sometimes you might not want to go out and have fun. An addendum to the story I opened this chapter with: The HNI wanted to go out the next night and bought even more bottles of Cristal. I was so tired around 10 p.m., I couldn't keep my eyes open. My wife looked so cozy in the bed. But I drank a few Dr. Peppers, left the house at midnight, and partied with the HNI until the club closed. You may think, "Well, I'd love it if that were my job," and if you're thinking that, I can tell you right now, you've never been there. What if, at that party, you had to commit the HNI to $1 million or you were going to go bankrupt? Would it be all fun and games? Or would it be work? I've had this pressure several times. I don't have a huge savings account. I'm what they call a "skin of my teeth" producer. So I have a little more motivation than others!

◇ Never over-promise. In an effort to make friends with an HNI, don't promise the world to him. I'm not talking about just your film here. I'm referring to things like, "I could get you into a Broadway show," and "I have a friend who could totally get you a deal on golf clubs." All of that is used-car salesperson bullshit. It also weakens the film investment, as if you had to give these "extra" incentives to make it a good deal. It's a great deal already! Promise nothing extra unless you can deliver 100%. Remember, you just gave him the opportunity and gift of a lifetime by letting him invest in your film. There's no reason to keep giving him things. And, if one of those promises you made falls through, he may start thinking you're full of it.

◇ Don't be afraid to ask hard questions. You're at a party and it's late and you're sure your investor is having a good time, but you need to be certain his radar has a blip for your project. Don't shy away from saying things like, "Hey, so we're cool to get you that contract tomorrow?" or "I'll have my lawyer draw up the paper and I'll meet at your office tomorrow." If he responds badly, then he wasn't a real investor.

◇ Be conscious of his feelings! If he's tired, don't keep him up. If he's happy, be happy too! If you have a producing partner and you feel the HNI likes him or her better, let it happen! You need to identify this and use it to your advantage. Make sure your partner is the point person. Don't let jealousy take over. At the end of the day, all that matters is the check.

Director Rob Iscove coaches
me and TV legend Betty
White before our dance scene
together in Love N' Dancing.

Final Thoughts

I also highly suggest reading any book on NLP (Neuro-Linguistic Programming), an ultra-effective tool that you can use to sell people on you. It's really amazing.

At the end of the day, you are always selling yourself. Remember that.

Also remember that you're giving the HNI a gift. You're letting him or her into an exclusive club. There's a cover charge.

TAKING ACTION

17

Reach for the Gold

At one point during all my motivational speeches, I use an exercise that illustrates the difference between wanting and doing. I say to the students, "Everyone wants, but no one does anything about it." The one thing that separates the successful people from the unsuccessful people is taking action. That's it. It's not intelligence, it's not talent, it's not education, it's not upbringing. It's the process of taking action.

I ask the students, "Everyone in here wants $1 million dollars, but how many of you are going to do something about it?" Then, to illustrate my point, I say, "I'm going to give you an example." I reach in my pocket and pull out a $10 bill. Remember, I'm talking to a range of kids from fifth graders to high school seniors, and usually it's in school districts that aren't well off, so $10 means something.

I hold up the bill and say, "Who wants $10?" Every hand goes up and there's a lot of excitement in the room. No one does anything though, except make a lot of noise and raise their hands. I repeat myself, "Who wants it?" Still nothing. So then I say, "I don't believe any of you! Come on... who really wants it?" Over the course of hundreds of speeches, it has never failed that (knock on wood) someone eventually runs up and grabs the $10 bill out of my hand.

I stop that student and make him say his or her name, as I grab my $10 back. I ask, "What did you do that no one else did?" The answer I'm looking for is, he or she got off his or her butt and took action! I tell that boy or girl, in front of the entire assembled crowd, that he or she will be a successful person one day because he or she does what no one else does: take action. Then I hand the student the $10 and ask the audience to offer a round of applause. Everyone gasps! (It's really funny what giving away money does.) I've proven my point: the difference between wanting and doing.

So I put it to you in this closing chapter. Imagine me holding a check for $200,000 or $3 million or $7.5 million in my hands. Are you going to grab it, or are you going to sit in the audience and watch someone else grab it?

If you sit there, that's fine. It will be a nice little story to tell your kids one day. "I tried to be a filmmaker, but it didn't work out." Kind of like that high school teacher everyone knows who could have been a professional ballplayer but "threw his arm out." Not a problem. He has a tale to tell for the rest of his life.

But, if you're like me, you don't want to tell stories. You want to be the story other people are telling. You want to be the one who runs up to the guy holding the check and grabs it. You can do it. You can get your film financed.

Take action.

Right now.

APPENDIX A

BOOKS FOR REVIEW

Bart, Peter and Guber, Peter. *Shoot Out.*
New York: Perigee, 2002.

    While this book will give you a general film industry overview, reading it doesn't excuse you from watching Bart and Guber's show on AMC.

Byrne, Rhonda. *The Secret.*
New York: Atria Books/Beyond Words, 2006.

Dyer, Dr. Wayne. *The Power of Intention.*
Carlsbad, CA: Hay House, 2004.

Hill, Napoleon. *Think and Grow Rich.*
New York: Tarcher/Penguin, 2005 (originally published in 1937).

    All three of these books create tremendous motivation and delve deeply into the amazing power of the law of attraction.

Bettger, Frank. *How I Raised Myself from Failure to Success in Selling.* New York: Fireside, 1992.

    My all-time favorite book on sales techniques, which is the key to financing your films.

Goodell, Gregory. *Independent Feature Film Production: A Complete Guide from Concept Through Distribution.*
New York: St. Martin's Griffin, 2003.

Schmidt, Rick. *Feature Filmmaking at Used Car Prices.*
New York: Penguin, 2000.

Simens, Dov S-S. *From Reel to Deal.*
New York: Warner Books, 2003.

    For producers and filmmakers, From *Reel to Deal* is the bible. No other book covers precisely what you need to learn to become a filmmaker. The other two books are fantastic as well.

Caine, Michael. *Acting in Film*.
New York: Applause Books, 2000.

O'Neil, Brian. *Acting as a Business, Third Edition*.
Portsmouth, NH: Heinemann, 2005.

These are my two favorite acting books, for different reasons. *Acting in Film* is just the best, most positive book on acting that I have ever read. Michael Caine starts from the assumption that you've already landed the role. I've read this book to motivate me nine times so far!

Acting as a Business goes over the nuts and bolts of being an actor and has started many careers, including my own.

Hall, Phil. *Independent Film Distribution*.
Studio City, CA: Michael Wiese Productions, 2006.

Keane, Christopher. *Romancing the A-List: Writing the Script the Big Stars Want to Make*.
Studio City, CA: Michael Wiese Productions, 2008.

Levison, Louise. *Filmmakers and Financing, Fifth Edition: Business Plans for Independents*. Burlington, MA: Focal Press, 2006.

Litwak, Mark. *Contracts for the Film & Television Industry*.
Los Angeles: Silman-James Press, 1999.

Simon, Deke. *Film & Video Budgets, 4th Updated Edition*.
Studio City, CA: Michael Wiese Productions, 2006.

Some producing books with specific information that may help you out in your quest of putting together a package.

APPENDIX B

WEBSITES AND OTHER RESOURCES

Entertainment Unions

These are the three unions with which, hopefully, you'll be working on all your projects:

Directors Guild of America: *www.dga.org*
Writers Guild of America, West: *www.wga.org*
Writers Guild of America, East: *www.wgaeast.org*
Screen Actors Guild: *www.sag.org*

Actor Research

www.sagindie.com is great site joining SAG and indie filmmakers.

Director Research

www.dga.org/dga_members/dir_members.php3 is an online searchable directory to find DGA member contact info.

Industry-Wide Research

www.IMDPro.com. I don't need to repeat how essential this paid subscription site is!

The Trades

As recommended, you need a subscription to one or both of these trade periodicals.

Variety: www.Variety.com
The Hollywood Reporter: www.Thr.com

Independent Film Crew and Vendor Research

www.Mandy.com
www.Mpe.net
www.LA411.com
www.NY411.com
www.Craigslist.com

Networking
www.thecircuitnyc.com will give you information about an excellent networking group in New York City.

Website Development
www.Bluegelmedia.com offers fantastic website templates to help you design your killer website.

Talent Agencies and Management Firms
All of the following talent agencies and management firms have their own film financing departments. Many not listed here have similar departments, so do your research, network, and find out how they can help you achieve your goals.

William Morris Agency
One William Morris Place
Beverly Hills, CA 90212
Phone: 310-859-4000

Creative Artists Agency (CAA)
2000 Avenue of the Stars
Los Angeles, CA 90067
Phone: 424-288-2000

International Creative Management (ICM)
10250 Constellation Boulevard, 7th Floor
Los Angeles, CA 90067
Phone: 310-550-4000

United Talent Agency (UTA)
9560 Wilshire Boulevard, Suite 500
Beverly Hills, CA 90212
Phone: 310-273-6700

Endeavor
9601 Wilshire Boulevard, 3rd Floor
Beverly Hills, CA 90210
Phone: 310-248-2000

Paradigm
360 N. Crescent Drive, North Building
Beverly Hills, CA 90210
Phone: 310-288-8000

The Collective
9100 Wilshire Boulevard, Suite 700 West
Beverly Hills, CA 90212
Phone: 310-288-8181

ABOUT THE AUTHOR

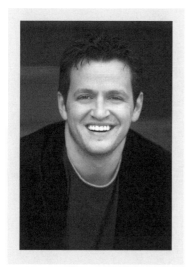

In 1998, TOM MALLOY was one of the lead actors in the film *Gravesend* produced by Oliver Stone. The film became an indie-cult favorite. When this film failed to make him a household name, Tom decided to learn as many facets of the movie business as he could. Over the course of eight years, he created his own method to finance films.

Tom first wrote and produced *The Attic*, a thriller directed by Mary Lambert (director of *Pet Sematary* and *Pet Sematary II*), and starring John Savage, Jason Lewis, Elisabeth Moss, and Tom.

Tom then wrote and produced *The Alphabet Killer*, a psychological thriller directed by Rob Schmidt (director of *Wrong Turn*). The film stars Eliza Dushku, Cary Elwes, Academy Award–winner Timothy Hutton, Michael Ironside, and Tom in one of the lead roles.

Most recently, Tom wrote and produced *Love N' Dancing*, a dance film/romantic comedy directed by Rob Iscove (director of *She's All That*). The film stars Amy Smart and Tom, along with Billy Zane, Betty White, and Rachel Dratch.

Tom is also a nationally-known motivational speaker. His message of "Making Positive Choices" has reached over 100,000 students.

www.TomMalloy.com
www.bankrollthebook.com

THE MYTH OF MWP

In a dark time, a light bringer came along, leading the curious and the frustrated to clarity and empowerment. It took the well-guarded secrets out of the hands of the few and made them available to all. It spread a spirit of openness and creative freedom, and built a storehouse of knowledge dedicated to the betterment of the arts.

The essence of the Michael Wiese Productions (MWP) is empowering people who have the burning desire to express themselves creatively. We help them realize their dreams by putting the tools in their hands. We demystify the sometimes secretive worlds of screenwriting, directing, acting, producing, film financing, and other media crafts.

By doing so, we hope to bring forth a realization of 'conscious media' which we define as being positively charged, emphasizing hope and affirming positive values like trust, cooperation, self-empowerment, freedom, and love. Grounded in the deep roots of myth, it aims to be healing both for those who make the art and those who encounter it. It hopes to be transformative for people, opening doors to new possibilities and pulling back veils to reveal hidden worlds.

MWP has built a storehouse of knowledge unequaled in the world, for no other publisher has so many titles on the media arts. Please visit www.mwp.com where you will find many free resources and a 25% discount on our books. Sign up and become part of the wider creative community!

Onward and upward,

Michael Wiese
Publisher/Filmmaker